MY BEAUTIFUL DARK '

Praise for the

It was only a matter of time before a clever publi
for whom *Exile on Main Street* or *Electric Ladyl*   ... and worthy of
study as *The Catcher in the Rye* or *Middlemarch* ... The series ... is freewheeling and
eclectic, ranging from minute rock-geek analysis to idiosyncratic personal celebration
— *The New York Times Book Review*

Ideal for the rock geek who thinks liner notes just aren't enough
— *Rolling Stone*

One of the coolest publishing imprints on the planet — *Bookslut*

These are for the insane collectors out there who appreciate fantastic design,
well-executed thinking, and things that make your house look cool. Each volume
in this series takes a seminal album and breaks it down in startling minutiae.
We love these.

We are huge nerds
— *Vice*

A brilliant series ... each one a work of real love — *NME* (UK)

Passionate, obsessive, and smart — *Nylon*

Religious tracts for the rock 'n' roll faithful — *Boldtype*

[A] consistently excellent series — *Uncut* (UK)

We ... aren't naive enough to think that we're your only source for reading about
music (but if we had our way ... watch out). For those of you who really like to
know everything there is to know about an album, you'd do well to check out
Continuum's "33 1/3" series of books — *Pitchfork*

**For reviews of individual titles in the series, please visit our blog at 333sound.com
and our website at http://www.bloomsbury.com/musicandsoundstudies**

**Follow us on Twitter: @333books
Like us on Facebook: https://www.facebook.com/33.3books**

For a complete list of books in this series, see the back of this book.

For more information about the series, please visit our new blog:

www.333sound.com

Where you'll find:

– Author and artist interviews

– Author profiles

– News about the series

– How to submit a proposal to our open call

– Things we find amusing

My Beautiful Dark Twisted Fantasy

Kirk Walker Graves

Bloomsbury Academic
An imprint of Bloomsbury Publishing Inc

B L O O M S B U R Y
NEW YORK • LONDON • OXFORD • NEW DELHI • SYDNEY

Bloomsbury Academic

An imprint of Bloomsbury Publishing Inc

1385 Broadway	50 Bedford Square
New York	London
NY 10018	WC1B 3DP
USA	UK

www.bloomsbury.com

BLOOMSBURY and the Diana logo are trademarks of Bloomsbury Publishing Plc

First published 2014
Reprinted 2014, 2015 (twice), 2016 (twice)

Library of Congress Cataloging-in-Publication Data
Graves, Kirk Walker.
My beautiful dark twisted fantasy/Kirk Walker Graves.
pages cm. – (33 1/3)
Includes bibliographical references and index.
ISBN 978-1-62356-542-8 (pbk.: alk. paper) 1. West, Kanye. My beautiful dark
twisted fantasy. I. Title.
ML420.W452G73 2014
782.421649092–dc23
2014000899

ISBN: PB: 978-1-6235-6542-8
ePDF: 978-1-6235-6458-2
ePUB: 978-1-6235-6770-5

Series: 33 1/3, volume 97

Typeset by RefineCatch Limited, Bungay, Suffolk
Printed and bound in the United States of America

For Whit

I have never seen a greater monster or miracle in the world than myself.
– Michel de Montaigne

Contents

CONTENTS

Acknowledgments

This project would not have been possible without the generous good faith of David Barker, Ally Jane Grossan, Kaitlin Fontana, and the rest of the 33⅓ team at Bloomsbury Academic. For her love and steadfast tolerance throughout the writing process, I owe my wife Jessica Graves a student-loan-sized debt of gratitude. Our son Whit was born squarely in the middle of the project, and I could not have asked for a more wonderful way to procrastinate. Many thanks are also due the Haley family – whether serving up a delectable paleo meal or hosting a lost weekend of Netflix binging, the good people of 1021 Emily Drive were always there to put wind in my sails, and I'm proud to be part of their tribe. Thanks also to my sister Lori for the many years of encouragement, patience, love, and support. Last but certainly not least, my late mother Dean Graves was my earliest critic and reader. I miss her sweet blandishments, her kind smile, and her soft-spoken enthusiasm to read whatever I was working on. And though I cannot fathom an afterlife scenario wherein she embraces the music of Kanye West – especially the songs on *My Beautiful Dark Twisted Fantasy* – I know she remains, eternally, my biggest fan.

Track Listing

Seven Virtues of Yeezus, Pop Christ

And the faithful congregated on street corners outside lofts, in parking lots near the city stadium, shuffling their feet over wet asphalt in the late spring darkness so as to arrive at the chosen place by the appointed hour. When Yeezus saw the crowds, he went up on the mountain, and he began to teach them.

Innocence
I'm forever the 35-year-old 5-year-old. I'm forever the 5-year-old of something.

Self-Possession
One of the problems with being a bubbling source of creativity – it's like I'm bubbling in a laboratory, and if you don't like put a cap on it, at one point it will, like, break the glass. If I can hone that…then I have, like, nuclear power, like a superhero, like Cyclops when he puts his glasses on.

Transcendence
Visiting my mind is like visiting the Hermès factory. Shit is real. You're not going to find a chink. It's 100,000 percent Jimi Hendrix.

Perspective
When I think of competition it's like I try to create against the past. I think about Michelangelo and Picasso, you know, the pyramids.

Wisdom
If you read books – which I don't, none at all – about how to become a billionaire, they always say, "You learn from your mistakes." So if you learn from your mistakes, then I'm a fucking genius.

Repentance
I spend more time watching porn and praying about it afterwards. Then I'll put on some Louis Vuitton and leave.

Forgiveness
[My Beautiful] Dark [Twisted] Fantasy was my long, backhanded apology. You know how people give a backhanded compliment? It was a backhanded apology. It was like, all these raps, all these sonic acrobatics. I was like: "Let me show you guys what I can do, and please accept me back. You want to have me on your shelves."

During a November 2010 *Today Show* interview with Kanye West, there is a telling moment when host Matt Lauer – redoubtable Matt Lauer, *sine qua non* of the affable, non-threatening American male – talks about regret and transgression. "And you're sorry," he says, nudging Kanye towards a full-throated apology for his nationally televised 2005 remark that "George Bush doesn't care about black people," spoken during a telethon in the wake of the federal response to Hurricane Katrina. Lauer had recently spent over three hours interviewing the former president upon the publication of *Decision Points*, Bush's presidential memoir. He tells Kanye the former president reserved his most emotionally piqued response not for questions about the Iraqi invasion, the federal bailouts, or the 9/11 attacks, but – amazingly – for a question about the boisterous thirty-something rapper. "Don't even listen this time," Lauer says, running the clip again. "I want you to just look at his face." The clip shows a saturnine Bush mouthing the words *"I resent it, it's not true, and it was one of the most disgusting moments of my presidency."* Kanye's body assumes the crumpled defensive posture of a publicly scolded child. Lauer gazes at him with tender opprobrium, looking like nothing so much as a man selling absolution for pennies on the dollar. Kanye considers the nudge for what it is, mentally tries it on for a moment like an ill-fitting Prada loafer, then balks and makes Lauer and everyone watching feel ill-fit for their own skin. "Yeah, I'm sorry for...mmm," he mumbles, unable to finish. Lauer looks on with the deadpan mortification of the decent and anonymous masses. "I think I get the point," he says.

Portrait of the Monster as a Young Masterpiece

Lurking somewhere amid the tabloid covers and reality show cameos, in the icy silence between tweets, the periods of relative calm preceding fresh bouts of histrionics, lost within the noxious cultural static that clings to his very name, there has always been – in spite of his best efforts to distract us – the music. And in the first decade of the twenty-first century, Kanye West created the best – the most consistently ambitious and thrilling – pop music of any American artist, hip-hop or otherwise, during the period. From "Through the Wire" – the first single off his 2004 debut LP *The College Dropout*, and the cockiest anthem of survivor gratitude this side of disco – to "Lost in the World," the penultimate track on 2010's *My Beautiful Dark Twisted Fantasy (MBDTF)*, more mystic dare than pop song – he has staked his claim as the digital era's first pop visionary, a multivalent talent with an intuitive genius for collage. Best known initially as Jay Z's wunderkind producer at the turn of the millennium, champion of the sample-driven "chipmunk soul" beats heard in "Izzo (H.O.V.A.)" and "Heart of the City (Ain't No Love)," West's music now illuminates the pop skyline with a gauche radiance all its own.

For sheer scale and visionary brio, *MBDTF* is his master-piece, the work that contains the fullest possible expression of his aesthetic vision. The album opens with a foreboding nursery rhyme chanted in a bad English brogue by rapper Nicki Minaj, and it ends with a relentlessly unanswerable question – "Who will survive in America?" – posed by late bluesologist Gil Scott-Heron, via a sample of his "Comment No. 1." Between those end stops lie sixty-eight minutes and thirty-eight seconds of closed-circuit narcissism, a buffet of sonic delights that blends rococo opulence ("So Appalled") with pornographic anxiety ("Hell of a Life"), suicidal ideation ("POWER") with feelings of omnipotence ("POWER"), redemptive humility ("All of the Lights") with go-for-broke ambition ("Monster"). The album unites disparate samples in a spirit of bold experimentation, incorporating prog rock as an enjambment here, transmogrifying a sixties radio pop melody into a hook there. Each song crackles with the intensity of a manic episode, employing every color in the sonic palette to paint a pop fantasia that is *sui generis*. *MBDTF* is such a testament to the power of first-rate American maximalism that one almost need look to literature – to twentieth century behemoths like *The Recognitions* and *Women and Men* – for an apt analogue. Simply put, the album has few peers in the way it stormed out of the gates and into the pop music canon.

That said, the 33⅓ series is devoted to landmark pop albums of the past few decades. Why write a book on an album less than four years old? How much perspective on the music is possible? In human terms, the average four-year-old has few tangible achievements outside toilet proficiency and a functional understanding of Velcro. And as music is such a vital force, a phenomenon as synonymous with life as respiration, shouldn't we apply developmental benchmarks to our judgment of its value? No sane person would presume to evaluate the legacy of a four-year-old. For most of the music we come to cherish, our love anneals in the crucible of elapsed time. The passing years trace the grooves in the culture the music has made, put our first impressions on trial in the courts of evolved taste and popular opinion. We hear, say, "Hey Ya" in an antiseptic department store lobby and receive deliverance across a lost decade, borne back to the moment of polymorphously perverse joy we felt upon hearing it for the first time. A truly great record is a miracle of double endurance, thriving in the besieged sanctum of the heart – beating back the *new music*, the competition for our ardor – while simultaneously persisting through time in the byzantine officialdom of critical acclaim. We reflect on where and when a particular record became more than a record, looking for the point at which the music's charm collided with our own tender susceptibility. We find meaning, prophecy, validation, and mystery in those points of connection. Time then bequeaths the music to posterity, cultivating the growth of an intergenerational democracy, a world where tomorrow's grandparents can share their grandchildren's burgeoning enthusiasm for *London Calling, Pet Sounds, The Chronic,* and *In the Aeroplane Over the Sea.*

The question, therefore, remains: Why write a whole book about such a young album? *MBDTF* is a concentrated dose of Kanye West, who, in his way, is a concentrated dose of the still-young digital era. Ours is a period of unprecedented and instantaneous access to books, films, fashions, and ideas. The vast majority of the world's recorded music is searchable and streaming, just a few clicks or swipes away. The arc of West's career reflects this digital ubiquity as no artist before him, the artistry of his samples a kind of transhistorical pop consciousness. And as the pop music canon continues to self-codify, new technologies have made it easier than ever to document and endlessly share our mandarin obsessions and revelations. Blogs and now apps have become clearing-houses for the kind of serendipity that dorm rooms and college radio stations used to provide. Kanye embodies our era's insatiable appetite to aggregate – to incorporate everything all at once – and *MBDTF* is the operatic sound of that insatiability set to music. To promote the album in the late summer of 2010, he even gave impromptu performances of new tracks at the headquarters of both Facebook and Twitter, where, at the latter, he opened his now infamous account.

There are many other compelling reasons to devote an entire volume to *MBDTF*. Few compete with the album's greatest theme, however, which is the saga of its creator's pathological need for greatness. More than a panegyric to excess or a celebration of his narcissism, *MBDTF* is a spiritual anatomy of Kanye West. Listen hard and you find that the fundamental conflict is between a child-emperor and his irrational fear of oblivion. "My-Beautiful-Dark-Twisted-Fantasy" – say it aloud. It could be the title of an essay penned by a vengeful third grader. The album is a portrait of genius held hostage on all sides by ambition, frustration, and insecurity, an allegory about art as the only valid response to emotional crisis and the only authentic mode of redemption.

If those descriptions sound a bit too highfalutin for a discussion about a pop star, that is because West is no ordinary pop star. In truth, it is unclear what he is, exactly, or what he might become. On *MBDTF* he often seems to bear more kinship to visual artists like Matthew Barney and Sigmar Polke than Lil Wayne or Prince.

From its swollen roster of diverse collaborators, to its polysemic tapestry of inspired samples and breathtaking hooks, to its creator's covetous wish to inherit the King of Pop's mantle, to the in-studio awareness during production of the stakes for West's career, to its yawping desire to sound like nothing else before or since, *MBDTF* is a monument to its own pursuit of perfection. For critics and fans across demographics, listening to the album once in its entirety was enough to ratify its status as an instant classic – more exploding quasar than landmark – but a classic nonetheless.

Because speculation about the motives of celebrities has become an unofficial American religion, and because he has so thoroughly knifed through most of the membranes separating self-promotion from self-expression, one could be forgiven for harboring suspicions that a critical study of Kanye West – one long overdue, in my estimation – might be nothing more than a PR stunt in essayistic garb on behalf of the rapper's camp. At this point it is worth mentioning that I have never met Kanye West. During my time spent preparing and writing the book, I have not attempted to contact anyone involved with the production of *MBDTF*, or any other West album, for that matter. Those among my digitally ambiguous circle of friends and acquaintants curious enough to inquire about my subject often looked askance whenever I told them. *What the hell for?* is what their well-intentioned looks of concern said, each flitting downward glance a courteous effort to shield me from pity or disgust. Even among my poptimist friends who approach records with the critical and evaluative rigor of Stephen Greenblatt, the idea of taking Kanye seriously for longer than the standard 750 word album review seemed extreme. In August of 2013, two months after the birth of his daughter North, Kanye was booed in Los Angeles at a Dodgers game when a jumbotron broadcast his image to the stadium's crowd. The incident was a metonym for his fraught status in popular American culture, a fitting counterpoint to his boast on the *MBDTF* track "Devil in a New Dress": "Hood phenomenon, the LeBron of rhyme / Hard to be humble when you stunting on a jumbotron." Unimpeachable as his musical output the past decade has been, the idea of what he represents – the odor of narcissistic aggression mixed with puerile vulnerability – is offensive to the general public. And though it may be tempting here to seek similarities to Michael Jackson, West's fallen idol, it is impossible to envision Michael so wholly polarizing the pop electorate at the peak of his career in 1985.

For these and various other reasons, writing in earnest about Kanye and his art poses certain challenges. The unofficial subtitle of this book, *A Theory of Kanye West*, speaks to what I openly and perhaps naively offer: a theory, a system of ideas – by definition imperfect, incomplete, and improvable – marshaled to make sense of something too complex for self-evident explanation. For whether or not we dare admit it, Kanye is an instantiation of the best and worst parts of, as he puts it, "living in that twenty-first century." Taking the measure of his music in light of that idea, we can discern in him some of the vital contradictions that shape our own experience, the same tug-of-war between the obsolete demands of analog life and the allure of digital ubiquity, of consuming and performing possibilities on every online platform, simultaneously, before an audience of virtually everyone. Narcissism is, after all, a mirror-making of the world. Looking into the two-way mirror of *MBDTF*, gazing upon its cipher of baroque embellishment, we may be surprised and even a little pleased at how familiar the grotesque reflection staring back appears when viewed at just the right angle.

The Narcissistic Personality
of Our Time

The May 2012 issue of *The Atlantic* magazine was the annual "Culture Issue" and two notable features received top billing. The first of these, the cover story ("Is Facebook Making Us Lonely?"), asks whether our vigorous online presence has made us lonely digital narcissists. The other feature ("American Mozart") profiles Kanye West, casting him as "the first true genius of the iPhone era, the Mozart of contemporary American music, intent on using his creative and emotional gifts to express the heartbreaks and fantasies of his audience." To open his Kanye piece, writer David Samuels relates an amusing anecdote about an exchange he had with President Barack Obama at a 2012 fundraising dinner in New York. "Kanye or Jay Z?" Samuels asks. "Jay Z," the president says. "Although I like Kanye. He's a Chicago guy. Smart. He's very talented." Samuels presses the issue, reminding the president he has publicly called Kanye a "jackass" in the past. "He *is* a jackass," replies Obama. "But he's talented."

That makes two consecutive leaders of the free world who, whether through provocation or professional courtesy, felt the need to comment publicly and on the record about Kanye West. What could possibly account for this? Had any pop musician in American history ever received public rebukes from back-to-back presidents? During the onset of the culture wars in the late eighties and early nineties, many congressional conservatives stridently denounced music deemed to be at odds with "traditional family values," but those attacks were largely of a political nature, not personal aspersions cast on the character of a particular artist. There are precedents for *good* pop star-presidential relations, of course, however improbable or bizarre. In 1970 Elvis Presley met with President Nixon in secret at the White House, where, astonishingly, he received a Bureau of Narcotics and Dangerous Drugs badge. For allowing "Beat It" to be used in a public service announcement campaign against teen drinking and driving, Ronald Reagan presented the "Presidential Public Safety Communication Award" to Michael Jackson in 1984. Scouring the past for a pop lightning rod akin to Kanye is a fool's errand, though, unless you expand the category of "pop stars" to include Middle Eastern dictators, in which case we can find numerous analogues.

Was it mere coincidence that the two features were juxtaposed in that issue of *The Atlantic*, an arbitrary editorial choice? Or did their proximity in an issue devoted to the zeitgeist symbolize a definite relationship, some indefinable link? What does the music of Kanye West have to do with loneliness and narcissism in the digital age?

Writer Stephen Marche opens his Facebook piece by recounting the ghoulish demise of Yvette Vickers, a former *Playboy* playmate in her early eighties found "mummified" in her Los Angeles home on April 27, 2011. She was believed to have been dead for nearly a year, her computer screen still aglow in the dim room where her body was discovered. A subsequent *Los Angeles Times* story reporting her death was shared thousands of times on Facebook and Twitter, a fact Marche deploys to vault into his examination of the relationship between loneliness and digital technology. "[Vickers] had long been a horror-movie icon, a symbol of Hollywood's capacity to exploit our most basic fears in the silliest ways; now she was an icon of a new and different kind of horror: our growing fear of loneliness," he writes. The feature proceeds apace with its big-canvas assessment, a lamentation for humanity's evolving incapacity for genuine connection. Marche is quick to poke his finger into the singularity – the throbbing contradiction at the heart of the article and the digital era's defining paradox: "We have never been more detached from one another, or lonelier," he writes. "In a world consumed by ever more novel modes of socializing, we have less and less actual society. We live in an accelerating contradiction: the more connected we become, the lonelier we are. We were promised a global village; instead we inhabit the drab cul-de-sacs and endless freeways of a vast suburb of information."

Tempting though it is to write off such a crescendo as manufactured editorial angst, the pop intellectual's equivalent of Glenn Beck crying on television while babbling about Woodrow Wilson and fascism, Marche is clearly on to something. Who among Facebook users with a shred of self-honesty can deny that the ceaseless comparison of life data between oneself and everyone else is spiritually vexing? Or that to experience Facebook at any given moment is to float atop a churning ocean of self-aggrandizement, self-promotion, and self-satisfaction? In *Infinite Jest*, his sprawling and prophetic novel of the digitized-to-death twenty-first century, the late David Foster Wallace coined a phrase that captures this unique brand of dysphoria: *the howling fantods*. As in, "My Facebook friend who now manages a hedge fund won't stop posting pictures of himself at Davos high-fiving Bill Clinton and Warren Buffet, and it's giving me the howling fantods."

There are as many variations on this theme as there are Facebook users, but the principle remains the same. As no technology before it, Facebook allows the average person a real-time means of inventing a public "self" – a manicured and attenuated ideal – within the voyeuristic imaginations of others. More a nexus of competing online public relations enterprises than a genuine virtual society, Facebook has become a legitimate mode of our being-in-the-world, whether we care to admit it or not. As Nicholas Carr notes in his bestseller *The Shallows: What the Internet Is Doing to Our Brains*, social networks have transformed "intimate messages – once the realm of the letter, the phone call, the whisper – into fodder for a new form of mass media...They've also placed a whole new emphasis on immediacy." The novelty of information disseminated via social media evaporates quickly, in other words, a fact that has institutionalized immediacy and newness as cardinal virtues of digital life. These twinned imperatives, to *make it new* and *make it now*, undergird the logic of information flow in the digital age.

Having evolved from the ethos of insatiable consumption that ascended unchecked during the postwar decades, we now have the 24-hour news cycle, "TV Everywhere" (the cable industry's mantra for feeding content to a subscriber's many screens), Google Glass, glib social anxieties like FOMO (Fear of Missing Out), self-rationalizing battle cries like YOLO (You Only Live Once), microblogs, cloud-based living, wearable tech, and a panoply of online platforms from which to build a digital following, or *tribe*, in the anthropological argot of the moment. Tiresome marketing hacks the world over chant their credo for our age at every opportunity: *Content is king.* If the fundamental creative criterion for a sixties artist of Bob Dylan's ilk was "to have something to say" – i.e., to offer oblique philosophizing or meaningful social commentary – today the imperative is simpler and much more literal: "Keep talking."

Along with the myriad conveniences that flow from intuitive digital technologies, our usage constitutes an unspoken acceptance of the associated psychosocial hazards. The conscious mind understands that Facebook is just a display case for life sculpture, a winnowing away of all that is not craft beer, precocious children, and the Ivy League. Yet the unconscious mind – the id for which immediacy is the only valid concept of time – is ill-equipped to provide perspective. Within the theater of our insecurities, appearance is very much the stand-in for reality. Whenever we look at Facebook some part of us, a very childish part, believes that what we see is what we get. By bearing continual witness to the nonchalant polish of other people's socially shared lives, we feel more remote from our own.

The idea that increased Facebook usage can engender loneliness in the user is now taken for granted, the workaday stuff of standup comedy and headlines in *The Onion*. Marche develops an argument in his *Atlantic* piece that explodes the cliché, though, by positing loneliness as one half of an essential contradiction in the American character. Noting that the Pilgrims who fled Europe "accepted [loneliness] as the price of their autonomy," cowboys on the frontier "traded away personal ties in favor of pride and self-respect," and the astronaut – "the ultimate American icon" – is nothing if not alone, Marche makes the case that loneliness is the inevitable obverse of self-reliance, that most exalted of all American ideals. The contradiction arises from the conflict between this type of lonely, iconoclastic individualism – which he likens to the Pilgrims' rebellion – and the oppressive herd impulse also native to the American psyche, the Salem witch trials "now read[ing] like attempts to impose solidarity." The implication is that, in opposition to the fabled instinct of pioneering entrepreneurialism, Americans also possess an unconscious will to enforce social integrity at all costs. In *Moby-Dick*, Melville finds a foreboding power within this psychic contradiction by invoking a geographic metaphor, inviting the reader to "consider them both, the sea and the land; and do you not find a strange analogy to something in yourself? For as this appalling ocean surrounds the verdant land, so in the soul of man there lies one insular Tahiti, full of peace and joy, but encompassed by the horrors of the half known life." Could it be that the oceanic instinct of our time, the unconscious psychic tide of the iPhone era, is the social adoption of the digital scale of values – superficiality, novelty, immediacy, self-immersion, connectivity, and conspicuousness? That the same society capable of producing the world's leading innovators and entrepreneurs has, in the process, laid the foundation for a culture fueled by digital narcissism?

The concept of pathological narcissism as a social affliction is nothing new. Christopher Lasch popularized the idea with his 1979 treatise *The Culture of Narcissism: American Life in an Age of Diminishing Expectations*. Diagnosing contemporary American life with narcissistic personality disorder, the book describes a society and culture obsessed with viewing reality in terms of a mirror:

> Notwithstanding his occasional illusions of omnipotence, the narcissist depends on others to validate his self-esteem. He cannot live without an admiring audience. His freedom from family ties or institutional constraints does not free him to stand alone or to glory in his individuality. On the contrary, it contributes to his insecurity, which he can overcome only by seeing his "grandiose self" reflected in the attention of others, or by attaching himself to those who radiate celebrity, power, and charisma. For the narcissist, the world is a mirror, whereas the rugged individualist saw it as an empty wilderness to be shaped to his own design.

Thirty-five years down the road, Lasch's diagnosis reads more like a prophecy of digital life than a critical analysis of Carter-era America. Especially with regard to the spell that celebrity has cast over the republic, the book's assessments have an eerie prescience. The narcissistic character of social media testifies to the way that personal celebrity has become a default aspiration. Literary critic David Shields comments on this phenomenon in his 2010 manifesto *Reality Hunger*: "The culture disseminates greater and greater access to the technology that creates various forms of media. 'Ordinary' people's cult of personal celebrity is nurtured by these new modes of communication and representation. We're all secretly practicing for when we, too, will join the ranks of the celebrated."

Twitter now stands as a legitimate sphere of public discourse and an important social barometer, an idea that only seven years ago would have been difficult to take seriously. While its value as a tool for social, even revolutionary, good was on full display during the Arab Spring uprisings of 2011 and the Iranian Green Movement protests of 2009, for a large percentage of users it's a conduit to the spectrum of celebrity. A live feed for personal opinions, one-two punch lines, banal and/or venal declarations, snarky *bon mots*, and staccato celebrity outbursts, Twitter grants anyone with an audience the ability to became famous (or infamous) – locally, nationally, globally – 140 characters at a time. Though the microblogging social network is much more than that, for our purposes its role as a trading floor for superficial exchanges and bursts of self-promotion is most important.

That metaphor – the stock exchange – captures the subtle ways social media has altered the nature of our relationships. Every status update, every tweet, every photo album, every blog post, every playlist shared socially via online music services like Spotify and Rdio – all of these choices are transactions. They impart information instantaneously and without friction, flowing inexorably across borders, an abstract but no less valid currency than the dollar or the yuan. They serve to purchase shares in an abstract but fully leveraged entity: your idea of *me*. Each social platform facilitates the trading process with some variation of Facebook's epoch-defining "Like" icon, allowing users to invest with a click of approval in content that pleases them, boosting that content's visibility and increasing its relative value to the poster's social portfolio. If, in the old analog days, "social capital" denoted one's accumulated professional and educational connections, the amount of "real world" influence a person was capable of wielding, it now signifies something much more complicated. In the iPhone era virtually everyone is a social capitalist, which is a less uplifting way of saying that we are all connected – searchable, streaming, optimized – whether we wish to be or not.

Once the concept of *influence* became the organizing principle by which to measure a person's digital celebrity, companies such as Klout, which assigns a numeric value to each user's social profile, emerged to brand the process. By satisfying the American appetite for rankings, Klout successfully appeals to its users' innate narcissism and thirst for personal celebrity. The company monetizes this celebrity by selling user data to marketers and advertisers eager to promote products to the influential. Social media platforms are thus not only sites of figural transactions, my purchasing *your* attention with compelling content to buy shares in an idealized *me*, but also literal transactions, wherein my personal data is sold to the highest bidder who will, in turn, attempt to sell me goods and services that flatter and meet the needs of my social profile. I respond to these surgically precise ads by purchasing items I find cool or useful, sharing my discoveries across multiple social networks, directly affecting the buying behavior of my friends, which – significantly – boosts my Klout score and level of social influence, capturing the attention of those same advertisers who purchase Klout data, and the narcissistic algorithm is repeated *ad infinitum*.

How do these twenty-first century dynamics relate to what Lasch perceived in contemporary American life circa 1979? In an early section of his book titled "The Narcissistic Personality of Our Time," he provides the underpinnings of his diagnosis: "Every society reproduces its culture – its norms, its underlying assumptions, its modes of organizing experience – in the individual, in the form of personality." At this point he delves into the murky intellectual waters of Freud and the psychoanalytic worldview, outlining the ways that each civilized society must try to solve "the universal crises of childhood" – separation from the mother, fear of abandonment, competition for mother's love, etc. The methods a society employs to confront these challenges determine to a large extent its characteristic personality, to which the individual submits and reconciles himself, careful to observe prevailing social norms. For Lasch, narcissism's migration from the realm of metaphor to the clinic represented a paradigm shift in the social personality type. Though an entire subgenre of self-help books on narcissistic personality disorder now exists (an Amazon search of books on "narcissistic relationships" yields over 1,000 results), at the time of Lasch's writing the clinical concept of narcissism was fairly new, having only been codified as a psychiatric disorder

in 1968. Obsessional neuroses and hysteria were the characteristic pathologies of Freud's day, extremes that mirrored the
social dynamics of early twentieth century capitalism,
including "acquisitiveness, fanatical devotion to work, and a
fierce repression of sexuality." The digital era has engendered
a set of pathologies that corresponds to the narcissism of our
daily routine, from the wall-to-wall screens we use to aggregate the fragmented world at large, to the social and commercial imperatives of strategic self-branding online, to the
virtualization of huge swaths of our lives. If Lasch is correct
that every era reproduces its culture (its products and its
pathologies) in the form of the individual, what does Kanye
West's status as superstar and pariah say about us? David
Samuels' "American Mozart" piece in *The Atlantic* was
anathema to many of its readers, prompting more than a few
longtime subscribers to renounce their allegiance to the
magazine. Was the outrage purely about offended sensibili-
ties, disgust at the various types of cultural miscegenation
(black and white, high art and low art, history and contin-
gency) implied in the comparison? Or was the response
about something more insidious and elusive, a repressed
recognition that the cultural ascent of Kanye's personality –
grandiose, egomaniacal, restive – was inevitable? That he is
not so much the voice of his generation as he is the narcissistic personality of our time?

Five Uneasy Pieces

At the Los Angeles premiere of his film *Runaway* in October 2010, Kanye West discussed artist George Condo's *MBDTF* album cover artwork with the unself-conscious exuberance of a child: "I told [Condo] I wanted a phoenix, and that's what he came up with. And what I love about it is, both me and George express ourselves with our truest vision, not based on what society or culture feels is right, but what's truly in our heart, and I just know if George was in my class back when I was in kindergarten, and he came up with something like that, I would've been envious, like, 'Man, how did you come up with that character with no arms and the wings, man? That's cool!'...And it's simply like that. I just really love the colors. I thought the colors were just amazing, and the imagery was amazing. I thought it was a cool, awesome cover."

Australian critic and *frieze* magazine co-editor Jennifer Higgie, in a 2007 essay on the art of George Condo ("Time's Fool"), describes his painterly universe as:

> [A] ribald world of crazed, comic engagement, theatrical illogic and a furious indifference to conventional niceties.

Lush, delicate swaths of paint delineate bodies penetrated by other bodies, pierced by objects ranging from harpoons and daggers to carrots, or plagued by mental disquiet; insanity is the order of the day, served with a side helping of sly cruelty...Traditional subjects such as reclining nudes and drunken men fuse with invented characters from prehistoric, Classical, or Pop culture, including slapstick Roman soldiers, snarling superheroes with beer bellies, demented saints wearing opulent robes and irate cave dwellers...But whatever the subject, every brushstroke seems to acknowledge the impact hundreds of years of painters – from Frans Hals and Edouard Manet to Otto Dix, Francis Bacon, Willem de Kooning and Phillip Guston (all painters to whom the physicality, the possibilities of paint, were as important as subject matter) – have had on Condo's technique, his exploration of space and his mind's eye.

Having burst forth from the East Village art scene of the eighties with fellow *enfant terrible* Jean-Michel Basquiat, Condo has spent the past thirty-plus years producing a visual lexicon of psychospiritual grotesquerie. The non-linearity of time plays a crucial role in his aesthetic (as Higgie writes: "I've never before wondered what might happen if a cavewoman was dumped in a 1920s' bar and thrown some lipstick and fishnets"), revealing a continuum of degradation in the anachronistic fissures. Condo's bizarre portraiture insists on depravity as the salient and transcendent characteristic of contemporary life, a style the artist himself has dubbed "artificial realism." A sinister aura informs the fictive personalities in his work, the product of a conflict between representational realism and a juvenile compulsion toward vandalism. Take a long look at, say, Condo's portrait *Batman and Bunny* (2005). Both the Playboy Bunny and Batman, icons of twentieth century American pop hegemony, are desecrated caricatures in the painting – *American Gothic* as seen from outside a photo booth in pop hell. Batman's cowl is an executioner's hood, and the visible outline of his mouth forms a horror-movie villain's gaping, deranged grin. One of the Bunny's eyes is bulging and blue, the other brown and demure; her nose is a bulbous pimple, her mouth a pentagonal graveyard for tombstone teeth. Her face looks like the work of a gruesomely Cubist plastic surgeon. If you stare at the painting long enough, you realize it's a portrait defacing two bloated and undead American fantasies. The effect is an embellished distortion of the kind sought by kids who draw Hitler mustaches and satanic horns on yearbook photos. The mangling is the message. The forms of physical derangement afflicting Condo's subjects – the asymmetrical eyeballs, the multiple mouths, the goofy impalements, the razorblade grimaces – emanate from the sensibility of some cosmically disturbed child. It isn't difficult to formulate a metaphor for Condo's sinister genius: Picture a preternaturally gifted brat with a flair for egotistic hyperbole, a contemptuous awe for human frailty (his own included), and a self-consciously refined aesthetic tuned in to pop's "the past is never dead" past. Sound like anyone we know?

On the album cover of *The College Dropout*, Kanye's 2004 debut LP, a forlorn bear mascot sits alone with slumped shoulders in the empty bleachers of a college gymnasium.

Clothed in baggy jeans, a T-shirt, and a corduroy jacket, the bear looks puzzled and depressed. A college mascot is generally an optimistic symbol, an icon of belligerent or eccentric goodwill evoking tradition, school spirit, and brand recognition. Representing what is both accessible and intangible – the communal masscult of athletics, on the one hand; the cartoonish abstraction of institutional identity, on the other – the mascot is shorthand for community. Ask any wayfaring alumnus or alumna what an image of an alma mater's mascot conjures, and the response is very likely to be earnest and sentimental. "Home," some will reply.

What to make, then, of Dropout Bear, the complexly ironic mascot adorning the cover of Kanye's first three studio albums? As a synecdoche for pop music's most notorious ego, an approachable teddy bear seems an odd point of self-reference. The fundamental datum of the Official Kanye West Biography is his decision in the late nineties to drop out of Chicago State University and pursue his musical ambitions. As success came, a personal mythology accreted around that fateful choice, culminating in the first album's title. Dropout Bear is a celebratory totem of the road not taken, the proverbial grin all the way to the bank. More than a biographic boast, though, Dropout Bear plays a significant role in foregrounding the psychic territory of Kanye's music. Look at *The College Dropout*'s cover art and imagine you've never heard of Kanye West. Who is this cipher in the bear suit, and why does he introduce himself to the world – honesty wearing an irony costume – under the banner of failure? A casual genius obtains in the idea of a loveable mascot for the world's college dropouts, a warm and fuzzy symbol of diffidence and disappointment. His major label debut LP – the fact of its existence – is Kanye's refutation of the middle-class rejoinder to "get your degree," his triumph in the face of conventional wisdom. Yet why does he define himself in the negative? Why do his first three albums loosely allegorize the college experience, something he necessarily eschewed, to tell his story?

Framing the image on *The College Dropout*'s cover is the kind of gilded border commonly associated with eighteenth century French painting, complete with singing cherubim and rococo flora. Has any debut album cover in the history of pop music ever captured an artist's basic contradiction with such exquisite honesty? This Beaux-Arts presentation of a grown man in a bear costume is quintessential Kanye, a just-so enmeshment of the ridiculous and the sublime. The cover is all poignant ambivalence, a conflicted attempt at simultaneous self-effacement and self-immortalization. Originally a token of his basic insecurity, the plush embodi-ment of his discomfort in the garb of Huxtable family values, Dropout Bear became a commercial trademark, Kanye West made cute and digestible. The evolution of the icon – from the physical costume worn for *The College Dropout*'s cover, to the Muppet-like figure dressed to the boarding school nines on the cover of *Late Registration* (2005), to the chromatically intoxicated "superflat" rendering by Japanese artist Takashi Murakami for the cover of *Graduation* (2007) – traces Kanye's musical evolution from cocky self-parodist (with an insecure shadow) to fully articulated narcissistic projectile. Murakami's artwork for the *Graduation* cover seems to play with this idea, depicting Dropout Bear – his education now complete – blasting into space. Over the span of just four years, the mascot shed its original ironic connotation only to gain a new one, as a postmodern anti-logo for a pop juggernaut.

Five different George Condo paintings commissioned exclusively for *MBDTF* became the album's five unique covers. The most notorious of the set is the one Kanye references *supra* in his interview with MTV at the *Runaway* premiere. In that painting a bare-breasted, armless phoenix with fangs, a Dalmatian tail, and angel wings straddles a naked West, who holds the telltale green bottle of the wino in his right hand. More than the armlessness of the mythological creature sexing him, the lecherous angles of Kanye's face are the most unsettling elements in the painting. Rather than an image of false contrition – something you might reasonably expect from a pop figure coming back from the 2009 West had – we get a debauched Yeezy self-portrait as refracted by Condo's brushstrokes. The unrepentant goblin on the blue sofa is the voice we'll hear in "Hell of a Life," a song that reimagines libidinal excess as a self-contained moral fantasy and means of social escape. Condo's genius for distilling the real through comically grotesque distortion – his puerile devotion to artifice and defacement – is on display here, but full of an odd pathos. Who can doubt that this painting captures a necessary and torturous contradiction in Kanye's creative soul, viz. a lewd acceptance of the worst parts of his nature for the sake of a painfully won authentic art? This particular cover more than any of the other four defines the dramatic arc of his evolution – from the rap nerd hidden deep within the bear suit of *The College Dropout* to the narcissistic exhibitionist having a fevered public wet dream – and visually sets the table for the listener's experience of *MBDTF*. A noncontroversial censorship controversy erupted when a pixelated version of the phoenix cover replaced the original in big box retail giants like Wal-Mart, prompting a series of Kanye tweets that compared the relative obscenity levels of Nirvana's (uncensored) 1991 *Nevermind* cover to Condo's painting for *MBDTF*. The pixelated phoenix cover has its own weird resonance, though, regardless of the retail and commercial considerations behind it. Like the final three minutes of vocoder distortion capping "Runaway," the pixelated Condo painting is a talisman of *MBDTF*'s – read: Kanye West's – relationship to digital ubiquity and digital exhaustion. The cover sighs "Why bother?" The large, colorful pixels are koan-like, articulating a non-articulable idea, begging the question of whether honest art is even possible in an age of continuous online presentation and performance anxiety, when every utterance and gesture is calibrated to slurp up maximum attention. Kanye's relationship to fame and celebrity is more fraught than anyone else's in pop or hip-hop today, and the pixels evoke a sense of defeat at the digital hands of overexposure.

The four other Condo cover paintings compel in unique ways. The famed ballerina painting (discussed in this book's "Runaway" chapter) is the album cover that greeted consumers who purchased the CD. Condo's Cubist depiction of West's head as a funhouse attraction, a hive of yapping mouths, is surely the most ingenious representation of a pop star's fractured ego ever conceived. The cover features an engorged head that eats up all the space in the frame. Kanye's eyes are stricken by Condo's signature asymmetrical affliction, with the roundly bloated right eye set to pop out of its socket. The rectangular spaces filling each open mouth look variously like the interior of a coffin, the proscenium of a black box theater, an empty diorama box, and a guillotine. Some of the square-fit teeth are white, some are gold, all are nightmarish. The cover is an astonishing portrait of how the human ego might look if we could capture its likeness in a fractional moment of chaos. Which incarnation of Kanye is this supposed to be? Is this the suicidal genius weathering dark weeks of the soul in an icy bedroom, howling out *808s & Heartbreak* in the dead of night? Is it the mind of the interloper standing on stage with Taylor Swift that night in 2009, in the millisecond when the poison dart boos first began to penetrate his adrenaline barrier? Perhaps this is the schizoid voice that tells the story of "Blame Game?" The cover's berserk intransigence, its simultaneous openness and resistance to interpretive perception, is why it captures the spirit of *MBDTF* better than any of the other Condo works.

The remaining two covers are similar enough to be easily confused. One is a picture of Kanye's decapitated head (which wears a king's crown) lying sideways on the ground, impaled by an upright sword, eyes open and fixed on death. A pleasantly azure sky with wispy white clouds embraces the scene. The final cover features the same sword plunged into a grassy hillock, with just the crown to keep it company. Neither Kanye nor his head are anywhere to be found. Of course, if the aughts taught us anything, it's that the absence of evidence is not the evidence of absence, or something along those blurred lines. The narcissist has left the building, in other words, but it's all right – he's in the bloodstream.

Art as Atonement

For all his presumptions of being misunderstood, Kanye West has received more critical adoration over the course of a decade than most artists will find in a lifetime. In the lead-up to the deafeningly overhyped debut of *Yeezus* (2013), his sixth studio album, the *New York Times* featured him on the cover of its Sunday Arts section ("Behind Kanye's Mask") for an interview. The accompanying image of West, snapped by fashion photographer Nick Knight, speaks volumes. Wearing a red balaclava, thick gold chain, and high-end black T-shirt, his arms crossed and his eyes closed in the deliberate manner of someone affecting impatience, he looks more like a petulant character from Wes Anderson's cutting room floor than a self-styled agit-pop provocateur – maybe a stowaway fashion student on Steve Zissou's ship with dreams of becoming a mercenary. Yet the mere fact of his presence on the front page of the Sunday *Times* Arts section signaled a crucial shift in his relationship to the public, an improbable point at which his untethered narcissistic sensibility had found a wider audience eager to call it art.

Writer Jon Caramanica spent three days interviewing Kanye about his nebulous extra-musical ambitions, the arc of his career, and the new direction indicated by *Yeezus*, a bleak drive down an electro-nihilist autobahn that West describes as "aspirational minimalism." As Caramanica notes in his excellent introduction to the interview,

> No rapper has embodied hip-hop's often contradictory impulses of narcissism and social good quite as he has, and no producer has celebrated the lush and ornate quite as he has. He has spent most of his career in additive mode, figuring out how to make music that's majestic and thought-provoking and grand-scaled. And he's also widened the genre's gates, whether for middle-class values or high-fashion and high-art dreams.

The interview turns particularly fascinating in the discussion of *MBDTF* and the impulses behind its creation. West describes the album as "a long, backhanded apology" made to regain his place on the shelves of an alienated audience. "That was the album where I gave people what they wanted," he says. Caramanica counters with the question, "Does that make *Dark Fantasy* a dishonest album in some way?", to which Kanye replies with a few bumbling ideas about the inevitable compromises of all visionaries and an implicit self-comparison to Steve Jobs, finally declaring that his sense of *MBDTF* as a compromised record is an example of his "never being satisfied."

Throughout his career, one of the most appealing and appalling parts of Kanye's persona has always been the doubleness of his ego – a weirdly complicated childish streak that charms and disgusts in the space of a single gesture. Watching footage from the infamous 2005 Katrina relief telethon, you can measure the shakiness in his voice with a seismograph. What he wants to do, his shaky voice tells us, is gather up all of the floating corpses and detritus and outrage in New Orleans, smash it into a bolus of righteous indignation, and fling it splattering into the living rooms of an ignorant and apathetic public. What he does is something different. Rather than bear witness to a moment of political courage by a precocious pop star, we see an embarrassingly inarticulate person who, though he yearns to say something meaningful about racial inequality and America's permanent underclass, talks instead about feeling guilty for shopping. That tension – a struggle between self-rationalized good intentions and reckless execution – is an animating force in West's life and music. So much so, in fact, that in spite of the status he enjoys as beat maven and rap genius, a plurality of the American public associates his name not with a corpus of inspired baroque rap futurism, but with two high profile and incendiary incidents that occurred during live TV broadcasts. The first of these, call it the "Bush Push" (mentioned above), was an unsolicited verbal sucker punch to a sitting U.S. president. The second incident was, of course, the buffoonish hijacking of Taylor Swift's acceptance speech at the 2009 MTV Video Music Awards. His intentions were, once again, avowedly noble – you see, he stole Swift's spotlight to shine it on the more deserving art of *someone else* (Beyoncé). He was the corrective principle of the pop universe, he was deconstructing the tastelessness of award shows, he was etc, etc, etc. The stunt was a bridge too far. The Taylor Swift brand is a sacred force in the marketplace, an ocean of commodified self-regard for millions upon millions of tweens, teens, and twentysomethings around the world. The outburst was self-destructive on a spectacularly visible scale, and in his usurpation of an otherwise unremarkable moment, he may have permanently alienated an entire generation of women. For those who already found his records distasteful, his antics proved his music to be the bombast of a narcissistic clown, the meretricious noise of a child drunk on his own Kool-Aid. His reputation grew to accommodate a host of social grievances, from incivility to race baiting to celebrity entitlement. The worst moment of his public life got its own meme on the Internet, when people across the globe began digitally superimposing his image on unrelated photos, captioning each one with some variant of his infamous interruption ("Imma let you finish, but..."). After an August during which political antagonism over healthcare reform became a blood sport in town hall meetings across the country, Americans found a vital center in their shared disgust at West's behavior. Watching his stillborn come-to-Jesus moment with Jay Leno a few days after the incident, it was clear that for Kanye West, atonement would require a lot more than penance. It would take a miracle.

More than any other poet of spiritual exile, Dante gave the world its most elegant rationale for *taking time to figure shit out*: "Midway through the journey of our life / I found myself within a forest dark, / For the straightforward pathway had been lost." No less than Don Draper, the wayward enigma at the heart of *Mad Men*, meditates on those first lines from the *Inferno* while sunning on a beach in the show's sixth season. And why not? The image endures down through the ages as a catechism of what it means to be human, a sentient and mistake-making creature adrift in the chaos. Given his compulsion for grandiose analogy, and his positive genius for self-deporting from the straightforward path, the image of Dante's wanderer is a fitting one to describe the state of things for Kanye following the Swift debacle in late 2009.

Complex magazine editor-in-chief Noah Callahan-Bever became a Kanye confidante over the years, and in early 2010 West invited him to spend time at Avex Honolulu Studios in Oahu, where *MBDTF* was recorded. Since a prophetic 2002 profile in *Mass Appeal* magazine (where he describes West as "hip-hop enough to appeal to the most thugged-out cats, but thoughtful enough to resonate with the underground"), Callahan-Bever has charted West's trajectory through the cultural ecosystem, providing anecdotal glimpses into an inscrutable psyche. For the November 2010 *Complex* cover story "Project Runaway," he provides an indispensable eyewitness account of the process by which our era's most dynamic pop star conceived his magnum opus.

Recounting a phone call with West in mid-October 2009, he writes: "Kanye West was over it, he said. Done with music. He'd clearly needed a break, and his subconscious had manufactured one. Now, he was all about fashion – red leather, gold details, and recapturing the decadence of late-'90s hip-hop in design. While I encouraged his pursuit since he was so obviously enthused, I confessed that it'd be a bummer if he abandoned music altogether." West was calling from Milan, having left the country following the Leno appearance. He spent a few weeks in Japan before jetting to Rome, where he began an internship at the Italian fashion house Fendi. Reminded of the trying circumstances behind the creation of the Rolling Stones' greatest LP *Exile on Main Street* in the south of France, Callahan-Bever admits he was intrigued by the possibilities of Kanye abroad. After a few months with little real communication, he received a brief email in January 2010 from the expat rapper: "Yooooooo, happy new year fam. I can't wait to play you this new shit!!!!" By late March, Callahan-Bever was "at Avex Honolulu Studios, the seaside recording studio on Oahu where West tracked [fourth studio album] *808s [& Heartbreak]*" and where he had block-booked "all three session rooms, 24 hours a day" until he was satisfied that the new album was complete.

One of the joys of reading NCB's piece is his clear-eyed rendering of both the process and the stakes interwoven in the album's production. He recounts matter-of-factly the hypomanic rhythms of West's machinations:

> Meanwhile, Kanye stares at his laptop, jumping between email and 15 open windows of art references in his browser. He polls those assembled on how risqué is too risqué for his blog, and occasionally barks mixing orders at the engineer, tuning subtle parts of the beat – all without breaking eye contact from his computer. This is how he works: all-A.D.D. everything.

None of this is surprising to anyone who has listened to the album, which is as much about aesthetic transformations of manic energy as is it is about anything else. "During my five days in Hawaii," NCB writes, "Kanye never slept at his house, or even in a bed. He would, er, power-nap in a studio chair or couch here and there in 90-minute intervals, working through the night. Engineers remained behind the boards 24 hours a day." Even more compelling is NCB's account of the shared awareness among the production's many players:

> But mostly we talk[ed] about Kanye's album: what it has to mean, and what it has to accomplish. At its heart, beyond the beats or rhymes, this conversation is the reason we were all summoned to the island (no *LOST*). It's never explicitly discussed, but everyone here knows that good music is the key to Kanye's redemption. With the right songs and the right album, he can overcome any and all controversy, and we are here to contribute, challenge, and inspire.

Callahan-Bever expresses an unpretentious wonderment at getting to participate in "Rap Camp," the playful moniker he gives to his time embedded in the album's production. Likening the experience to a camp – a clinic put on by some of rap's leading lights – makes a lot of sense. If you bother to take a census of the dozens of artists, producers, and engineers who worked on *MBDTF*, it's easy to forget you're not looking at the credits of a major motion picture. In addition to the sweeping scope of the production and the vivid after-images etched by its blaze of excess – the undeniable *visual* dimension of the surplus sonics – *MBDTF* feels like visual art in other respects, as well. The more one learns about the collaborative intricacies of the production, the more tempting it is to look at Kanye as director, as compositional auteur. To get at this idea, Callahan-Bever quotes legendary hip-hop producer Q-Tip, who was part of Rap Camp in Hawaii:

In art, whether it was Michelangelo or Rembrandt or all these dudes, they'll sketch something, but their hands may not necessarily touch the paint. Damien Hirst may conceptualize it, but there's a whole crew of people who are putting it together, like workers. His hand doesn't have to touch the canvas, but his thought does. With Kanye, when he has his beats or his rhymes, he offers them to the committee and we're all invited to dissect, strip, or add on to what he's already started. By the end of the sessions, you see how he integrates and transforms everyone's contributions, so the whole is greater than the sum of its parts. He's a real wizard at it. What he does is alchemy, really.

What Q-Tip describes is an update on the dusty divine-right-of-the-visionary idea, which holds that certain works of art owe their status *qua* art not to the hands that rendered the brushstrokes but to the presiding genius that commissioned them. Andy Warhol's Factory springs to mind, but so does Steve Jobs' Apple. Viewed in this light, Kanye's self-comparison to Jobs is less far-fetched. Jobs' singular genius lay in his capacity to creatively synthesize art, technology, and commerce – to unite disparate and ostensibly nonessential elements into products of transcendental beauty, eating up market share in the process. The iPod was certainly not the first portable MP3 player on the market, but it was the first to double as a functional art object. With its clean design and sleek aesthetic polish, it made an irresistible promise to transform an *activity* into an *experience*. We bear daily witness to Jobs' thought touching the canvas in the round corners and bright icons of our everyday devices. Like Jobs, Kanye places total faith in his aesthetic ego. His production ethos is one of frenzied collage, an ongoing wager with himself that he can refashion (and rebrand) whatever he finds – in the pop music past, in contemporary art, in haute couture – into manifestations of his creative narcissism (his "dreams," as he called them during mid-show rants on his 2013 *Yeezus* Tour).

As an art form collage is defined, of course, along literal lines of contradiction. In 1912 Picasso glued oilcloth on his canvas for *Still Life of Chair Caning,* bounding the elliptical work with a length of actual rope. By sampling the alien stuff of a foreign world, the world of everyday objects beyond the painting's borders, Picasso deepened the possibilities of the medium. From the heyday of Dadaism and Cubism onward, the most effective collagists, with materials as varied as industrial detritus, voicemail messages, and ATM surveillance footage, have used discontinuity to mirror indwelling ideas about art. Through collage, the artist insists on exemption from generic mandates and program-matic techniques, freeing himself to intuit undiscovered possibility. The importation of "foreign" material into a work of art, seen in this light, is less an act of disruption than one of correction: the slumbering sameness of expectation, the mirage of the world's veneer, is a necessary but limiting illusion. Only through the personal act of selective appropriation, the collagist asserts, can we find what we never knew we sought – the elusive pattern inscribed within chaos, the harmony encoded in noise. As a mode that celebrates fragmentation and obscurantism, is there a form of art more commensurate with life in the twenty-first century? *MBDTF* embraces this idea as a *cri de coeur*, performing a formal miracle in which brokenness of every sort is the only prerequisite for aesthetic rebirth.

University as Universe: *The College Dropout*

The arc of Kanye's first three albums – *The College Dropout, Late Registration*, and *Graduation* – traces the through line of a hip-hop bildungsroman, documenting the evolution of a precocious talent into a self-aware, voracious cultural ego. *The College Dropout* is the most uneven and charmingly immature of the three, full of the indulgent overreach so common in the first records, films, and novels of preternaturally gifted artists, and for that reason it makes an ideal counterpoint to *MBDTF*. The album title is an obvious reference to West's biography, specifically his decision to drop out of Chicago State University in the late nineties to focus on music production. As the son of a college professor mother (Dr. Donda West taught English at Clark Atlanta University) and photojournalist father (Ray West is a former Black Panther), Kanye was the product of middle-class aspiration. *The College Dropout* is the canvas on which he juxtaposes the contradicting figures of ambivalence and ambition at the heart of his early career.

Thematically the album stays true to those contradictions from the very first track ("Intro"), a sketch performed by comedian Deray Davis (doing an uncannily astute impression of Bernie Mac as a college administrator) entreating Kanye to whip up a song that will inspire class harmony and make "the kids" sing on graduation day. The song is "We Don't Care," a playful and sardonic meditation on how the deck is stacked against poor black youth in America. The ironic chorus is a singsong celebration of drug dealing as a form of supplementary income: "Drug dealin' just to get by / Stack ya money til' it get sky high." Constructed around a sample of the first few twinkling bars of "I Just Wanna Stop" by seventies funk act The Jimmy Castor Bunch, "We Don't Care" sets the tone for the rest of the record, a generous collection of songs that pulses with comic ambivalence. These are sanguine cuts full of a buoyant, youthful vigor that hedge between a heavy-handed lyrical cleverness and an earnest, transparent vulnerability. "All Falls Down," the album's second single, typifies this dichotomy. On the track we encounter for the first time one of the definitive Kanye contradictions – his simultaneous critique and celebration of his own self-conscious materialism. The song's hook is an interpolation of Lauryn Hill's acoustic "Mystery of Iniquity," and in the context of the verses it becomes a kind of melodic sigh of inevitability ("I'm telling you all, it all falls down"). Describing the plight of a clueless third-year college sopho- more content to hide from life on campus (while feeding her appetite for luxe), the first verse looks outward to paint a wryly critical portrait of a Kanye archetype, the "single black female addicted to retail." The song's third verse finds him turning the spotlight inward, offering an honest appraisal of his own compulsion to consume with the same recklessness as his sophomore: "I want to act ballerific like it's all terrific /

I got a couple past due bills I won't get specific." The official video for "All Falls Down" represents this self-consciousness with a formal conceit, using a continuous first-person POV from Kanye's perspective to document a walk through the airport with a shallow and materialistic girlfriend (played with convincing flightiness by actress Stacey Dash). At one point we see an earnest Kanye staring at himself in the mirror of a terminal bathroom, scrubbing mustard from his shirt as he raps about not being able to go in public without wearing stylish clothes. "All Falls Down" is an exercise in comic poignancy, showing us the world through the cocksure vulnerability of Kanye's perception, a perspective that captures something elusive about the fraught relationship between ego and society.

As a musician for whom the full-length album is still a viable *aesthetic* category – an increasingly rare pop commodity in the age of disposable one-click digital singles – Kanye excels at maximizing the LP format. Coming in at 21 tracks over a span of seventy-six minutes, *The College Dropout* bursts at the seams with sonic portraits of the artist as a young man. In the middle of the album, two tracks (when heard consecutively) paint an oddly touching and relatable portrait of youthful arrogance and aspiration. The first of these is a lovely abridged rendition of gospel standard "I'll Fly Away" sung with soulful doo-wop harmonies. The song that follows is "Spaceship" – a nostalgic daydream where unrecognized talent and unrequited love are identical. Like a few of the other standouts on the album, "Spaceship" derives its sonic texture from a soul sample (Marvin Gaye's 1973 "Distant Lover") whose howling Eros has been sublimated into egotistical striving. The first verse is a trip back in time to Kanye's experience working in a mall with a reference to the Gap. The song proceeds to highlight the indignities familiar to anyone who has ever worked a retail job – the asshole managers, the awkward de facto racism, the general malaise of malls. Where "Spaceship" transcends its own potential banality, though, is in the hook. The appropriated bits and pieces of "Distant Lover" create a melody that tiptoes toward the idea of escape, a measured ascent that traces the distance between the prison of facts and the freedom of fantasy. The hook works so well because it sounds like the inner logic of a reverie. Listening to it, you can almost see a wounded bird struggling to fly skyward in a convoluted helix. This kind of melodrama – the kind that has fun with its earnestness – is what gives *The College Dropout* its endearing glow.

With "Through the Wire," the album's signature track and lead single, a near tragedy becomes the basis of Kanye's first great Song of Himself. The facts surrounding the track's genesis have passed into the realm of pop legend: After leaving a recording studio in Los Angeles during the early morning of October 23, 2002, Kanye was involved in a head-on car crash near the W Hotel. Rushed to Cedars-Sinai Medical Center where his fractured jaw was wired shut, he wrote and recorded "Through the Wire" a mere two weeks after the accident. Punning on the title of the sped-up Chaka Khan sample ("Through the Fire") in the song's hook, "Through the Wire" is the joyful story of its own creation, a triumph of creative opportunism. Lyrically the song is a deft balance of self-effacing humor (rhyming "an Ensure for dessert" with "just sip the sizzurp") and self-serious morbidity (an allusion to Emmett Till), more of the sharply attuned comic ambivalence that defines so much of the album. By dramatizing the aesthetic principle that distinguishes Kanye's best music – its intuitive orientation toward possibility – "Through the Wire" possesses a sonic exuberance insepa-rable from its creator's. On the most obvious level, the song is an end zone dance by a hungry young artist poised for a breakthrough, an anthem to cheating death at the moment life is about to begin. (A useful context for just how much Kanye struggled before making it as a solo artist is given on *The College Dropout*'s final track, "Last Call," an oral history of nearly thirteen minutes.) In his choice of Chaka Khan's "Through the Fire" as a spiritual commentary on his own ambition, though, West transforms his song into something like a hymn to the human spirit. Where "Through the Fire" is a soulful ballad consecrating a hungry lover's perseverance, her relentlessness in the pursuit of her beloved, "Through the Wire" is a goofy love song to Kanye's future, to what his own egoism and vision will achieve. The track is a fusion of elements equally boisterous, personal, and fun, the embry-onic sketch of a career-to-be.

A (Very) Brief Aside Re: *808s & Heartbreak*

808s & Heartbreak (2008) is the most underrated album of its decade. The icy, cavernous netherworld of Kanye's stripped-bare fourth studio LP was broadly derided as an emotionally indulgent misstep. Critics and fans alike scratched their heads in confusion at the Auto Tuned vocals, the bleak sonic winterscapes, and the mournful lyrical gloaming that coated the whole affair. And, to be honest, the album *is* something of a self-pitying monologue performed in the dark, a grief counseling session with no grief counselor. Yet in spite of all that – *because of it* – 808s endures as an avant electropop masterpiece and a frozen reflecting pool of self-doubt. You can spend hours inside Kanye's five other albums and you won't find anything to approximate the unguarded intimacy, caustic despair, or emotional riskiness of this record. From the neurotic plaint of "Say You Will" to the flickering inflections of hope in "Street Lights"; from the danceable codependency of "Paranoid" to the android talking blues of "Bad News," *808s & Heartbreak* deserves a 33⅓ volume of its own. May it grace our shelves before too long.

My Beautiful Dark Twisted Fantasy

Dark Fantasy

How else do you kick off an album called *My Beautiful Dark Twisted Fantasy* except by fucking up a fairy tale?

> I guess you think you know this story
> You don't. The real one's much more gory.
> The phony one, the one you know
> Was cooked up years and years ago,
> And made to sound all soft and sappy
> Just to keep the children happy.[1]

The six lines above comprise the beginning of "Cinderella," a Roald Dahl poem from *Revolting Rhymes*, his 1982 collection of revisionist fairy tale spoofs. Dahl's version of the tale parodies the courtly romantic idealism of the original, transforming the eponymous heroine from a demure diamond in the rough into a shrill entitled wench. The prince in Dahl's poem is a homicidal sociopath, decapitating Cinderella's two hideous stepsisters in quick succession when they claim the lost slipper as their own. He calls Cinderella a slut and demands

---

[1] Roald Dahl, *Revolting Rhymes* (New York; Knopf, 1983), 1–7

her head, too, but – disillusioned with the toxicity of her own fairy tale – she makes a wish to her fairy godmother for a life of anonymous decency, far from the trappings of wealth and monarchy. She lives happily ever after as the hausfrau of a "simple jam-maker" in a home full of laughter and smiles. The poem makes *us* laugh and smile because it validates the confirmation bias of adulthood. The condescending voice in those first six lines drips with the cynicism of experience. The tale we learned as children was sanitized and distorted, a necessary fiction meant to mollify vulnerable psyches. Now, of course, we're old enough to hear the unpleasant truth, which – being adults who learn the hard way – we already know. Blind faith in the eventual triumph of perfect justice and true love is a dangerous delusion. (You can get beheaded!) The true fairy tale, the poem says, is a life free from the bondage of fairy tales, a quiet mind and a content heart. Dahl's comedy flows from the idea of someone ballsy enough to revise something so deeply interwoven in the culture – for what is a fairy tale if not just a petrified public wish? – along the lines of a private epiphany.

"Dark Fantasy" opens with an Auto Tuned gospel chorus of digitally altered angels filling the celestial space with "oohs" and "ah-ah-ah-aahs" while what sounds like a deranged English kindergarten teacher trying to harrow her classroom narrates a story that sounds, well, strangely familiar.

The voice we hear narrating belongs to rapper Nicki Minaj, interpolating the introduction to Dahl's "Cinderella" by twisting the language to suit this version, Kanye's version, of the fairy tale. "Dark Fantasy" is Kanye defining the distance between where he started and where he is, a strut from the wide-eyed Midwestern incredulity of *The College Dropout* to the glutted bloodshot narcissism of *MBDTF*. He delivers the song's opening bars with a defiant contempt, recalling his youthful fantasy to one day look at the world from behind the wheel of a Lamborghini Murcielago. The memory is quaint now, the car a nostalgic talisman of what he used to want. He wants greatness now – straight, no chaser – that's his version of Dahl's transformed "Cinderella" ending, the only antidote (he imagines) to his restlessness.

Because Kanye West is equal parts imagist and musician, a collagist whose primary medium happens to be music, a brief digression is necessary. Any thoroughgoing exploration of *MBDTF* has to take into account the visual textures of its sound. The best way to do this is by referencing *Runaway*, the thirty-five-minute short film he directed that doubles as a marathon music video. Bearing the same title as *MBDTF*'s keynote track, *Runaway* contains all of the album's maddening contradictions. It is self-mythologizing, rife with hubris, assertively "artistic" to the point of unintentional parody; it is also the work of a pop visionary, a rapturous fairytale-as-emotional-autobiography overflowing with sensual delights whose climax fields a fully choreographed ballet. Filmed on location in Prague, *Runaway* is West's egoism reimagined as art house cinema, a self-contained dream fugue that sublimates his personal saga into an opera of gaudy regeneration.

Opening with an image of Kanye sprinting down a dim forest path to a soaring excerpt from Mozart's Requiem Mass in D minor, the film announces itself as a baroque allegory of the album's creation. The tongue-in-cheek reading goes something like this: In the wilderness of his exile from the American mainstream, the disgraced pop genius discovers his muse to be nothing less than the fires of his own narcissistic ambition. Through a series of forays into the most exotic and far-flung locales in his imagination – leading to a fully consummated relationship between ego and id – the prodigal brat is reborn as the sonic maximalist destined to reclaim his rightful perch atop Olympus, a demiurge of decadence. Hence, *MBDTF*.

The film's principal conceit revolves around the relationship between Griffin (played by West) and a phoenix (supermodel Selita Ebanks), who – in the form of a fiery projectile from the heavens – collides with Griffin as he drives his MTX Tatra V8 sports car through an enchanted twilit forest. The heavy-handed mythological allusions here are commensurate with *Runaway*'s subject, which is, after all, the regenerative grandeur of Kanye West's ego. The track playing during the film's opening sequence is "Dark Fantasy," and the hook samples vocals (provided by former Yes lead singer Jon Anderson) from Mike Oldfield's dated 1983 spacewalk "In High Places." The voice in the sample is clambering toward heaven, embedded within a soaring chorus that critic Chris Richards ingeniously describes as "a mutant gospel crescendo." That crescendo is a gnostic swell of aspiration, the restive yearning of a man who fancies himself pop music's Alexander. The question the sampled voice asks in the hook – "Could we get much higher?" – is both rhetorical and earnest, a recognition of standing atop the highest mountain while pining for still greater peaks. As Griffin carries the phoenix in his arms away from the scene of the collision, his slow-motion silhou-ette emerges from the darkness as a firestorm billows skyward. The explosive image recurs throughout the film, a leitmotif and proxy for the artist's volatile ambition.

The bridge in "Dark Fantasy," sung by folk pop icon Justin Vernon of Bon Iver, contains some of the album's oddest and most intriguing lyrics: "At the mall, there was a séance / Just kids, no parents" and "Then the sky filled with herons / (I saw the devil) in a Chrysler LeBaron." To find this kind of inscru-tably suggestive surrealism in a rock or pop lyric, you need reference the Dylan of "Sad-Eyed Lady of the Lowlands" – the images here smolder with the same otherworldly dream sense. Coming late in a song that takes a preemptive victory lap ("Could we get much higher?"), the words summon the dread of a greensick tornadic sky, a portentous glimpse of the storm to come. That the devil makes an appearance here is signifi-cant, an adumbration of the cosmic psychodrama we're already witnessing. The firestorm that dominates the "Dark Fantasy" sequence in *Runaway* now assumes a wholly different aspect, a decadent holocaust that consumes Kanye from within. A primary component of his creative narcissism, the decadence is as much threat as asset – Faust and Christ in the same small room.

With this contradiction in cryptic high relief, *MBDTF* unveils its high wire act of impossible tensions.

Gorgeous

That *hook*.

From the cold-open instant of its first shimmering reverberation, the bitches brew hook embodying the song's title sweeps us into the drama of "Gorgeous," Kanye's cultural vendetta and scattershot mission statement for *My Beautiful Dark Twisted Fantasy*. As the second track on the album, it arrives with the fully formed abruptness of lightning before thunder, a score-settling swagger that draws a clear line between the miracle of this moment's excellence and everything that came before. Sewn together with the indelible hook crafted by Kanye collaborator Kid Cudi – built from the sample of a yearning guitar melody in the Turtles' 1969 hit "You Showed Me" – "Gorgeous" is a methodic mountain climb up the north face of Mount Olympus. In as much as *MBDTF* was, by design, the work of art that would redeem Kanye in the public imagination, "Gorgeous" sets the album's stakes. The song is a relentless push of lyrical dexterity and Kanye's finest moment as an MC.

What's to love about "Gorgeous?" An obvious point of departure is the modulation of Kanye's voice, a tinny divination from within a Campbell's Soup can floating through interstellar space. The effect lends urgency to the lyrics and reinforces the notion that the track is a transmission from a faraway realm, a dispatch from the future or the surface of the sun. The layers of sound in "Gorgeous" – which, despite its intentional strutting, is the soberest track on an album intoxicated with its own grandiose neuroses – are lush and fecund enough to overload the brain's pleasure center. A melodic piano chord romances a monomaniacal electric guitar riff while full-bodied cellos sway seductively in the background. The guitar riff is the earworm here – that trans-figured snippet of sound from 1969 – and it sounds like a dance craze for brooding obsessive-compulsives, three steps forward and one step back. The light percussion that steadies the ship is so subtle as to go unnoticed, keeping its head down while pop's moody captain delivers his soliloquy on the quarterdeck.

Kanye takes a lot of heat for presenting such a perpetually self-serious scowl in public, and the question of whether or not he has a functional sense of humor remains open. The 2009 "Fishsticks" episode of *South Park* left no doubt about its writers' opinion, depicting him as the only person in America who doesn't get a crude joke that becomes a wildly popular national phenomenon. Narcissistically refusing to allow anyone to explain the dimwitted joke to him (he self-identifies as a "genius" and "voice of a generation" throughout the episode), Kanye stubbornly insists on decoding it for himself. The episode ends with him misinterpreting the punch line in such an egregious fashion that his whole iden-tity is altered, and he sets out to begin a new life as a "gay fish."

Though I generally find topical *South Park* episodes strident and unfunny, "Fishsticks" is brilliant. The idea that Kanye's ego is *a joke he can't decipher*, a punch line that any buffoon on the street recognizes as hilarious but that Kanye can't make head or tail of, resonates with anyone who's ever paid attention to his interviews, his antics, his Twitter feed, or his lyrics. In articulating that notion through humor (always the most efficient delivery system for a complex idea), the "Fishsticks" episode offers an inadvertently empathetic portrayal of how confounding the world must often be to a bona fide narcissist. Kanye's pride has, in moments, erected barriers meant to protect the sanctity of his rigidly inscrutable intentions (cf. the self-detonated *Today Show* interview described *supra*), the result of which is a stalemate between the genius of his ego and the opprobrium of the public. "Gorgeous" is a chink in those walls allowing light to spill into the psychic dark, and the rewards of a close listen pay huge dividends in understanding.

The hook's lyrics are the first we hear, delivered by guest collaborator Kid Cudi, and they set the table for the rest of the album. Man-on-the-verge phrases like "I can feel it slowly drifting away," "I'm on the edge," and "I will never ever let you live this down" suck the oxygen out of the song's antechamber, and Kanye's delivery occurs in that state of menacing breathlessness, a polemic that barely escapes.

The ambiguity of who is speaking in the hook – a type of figurative ventriloquism – is an important motif on *MBDTF*. Throughout the record Kanye indulges in certain impulses, moods, and reflections via the remove of a collaborator's voice. The hook's lyrics serve as a complicated emotional confession of deepest turmoil. In it, we get Kid Cudi performing the central anxiety at the album's core, the reimagined affirmation in Kanye's mind that everything depends on *MBDTF*. An overpowering prescience that the result will be binary, deliverance or destruction, haunts the refrain, calling to mind images of imminent threat – a plunge from a great height, perhaps, or an undertow sweeping him away from shore. "I will never ever let you live this down, down, down" is an intrusive and unwanted thought, a vague recrimination whose origin is untraceable, words that could plausibly come from anyone – Taylor Swift, George Bush, Kanye himself.

The first verse is a flawlessly delivered onslaught of embittered cool, wherein Kanye aligns the righteousness of his return with his indignation at institutionalized racism. Two phrases – "penitentiary chances" and "inter-century anthems" – are the organizing principles. The first four bars – outlining the "penitentiary chances" of the urban poor – transcend the familiar hopeless sigh at the drug game's death grip by interlocking with the next five bars (which define institutionalized racism as a social branding campaign) to decode a chain of historical consequences. The term "branded" is a doubly pejorative allusion to (and conflation of) the old wounds of slavery and the new wounds of marketing demography. The hip-hop "anthems" that glorify lawlessness, violence, misogyny, and materialism are less the result of reflected realities than the wholesale branding of "black urban despair" as a market category. (Kanye will pick up this thread again, albeit with much more clumsiness and rage, in "New Slaves" on 2013's *Yeezus*.) The inner city "Jeromes" who buy into the category and aspire to live its lie wind up behind bars, while the "Brandons" of the world, the kids who listen to the "anthems" from a safe suburban remove and who form a false identification with the music's images, get off with light sentences when push comes to shove.

Kanye delivers every word of every bar in "Gorgeous" with an icy determination and numb conviction in the track's principles. The second and third verses showcase a host of unforgettable metaphors, viz. hip-hop as the language of a new religion, the "soul music" desperately needed by the de facto "slaves" of a new era; *MBDTF* as a "road to redemption"; the fusion of Kanye with Malcolm X in a pop stew; Kanye as a "black Beatle." The first time I heard the "black Beatle" line, I wondered who had made such an invigorating comparison. Googling it, I learned that – who else? – Kanye had. The plosive conviction of his delivery makes the analogy, in the thrill of the moment, a fact. "Gorgeous" amends the old adage to claim that *being great* (more than living well) is the best revenge. He even settles the score with *South Park* when he imagines choking one of its writers "with a fishstick," recycling the show's crude pun ("fish dick") as an insouciant afterthought. The self-appropriated Malcolm X mantle is one we first encountered in "Good Morning," the intro track off *Graduation*. In that song Kanye boasts about being a fashion-forward update of Malcolm, less an obnoxious trivialization of the icon's legacy than a silly nod to West's own value system (i.e., the clothes very much make the man). By the time of *MBDTF*, though, the invocation of Malcolm X is no longer a clever joke; it's a bold assertion of cultural identity.

Rhetorically asking whether hip-hop is an encoded new religion – stylized reincarnations of slave spirituals – Kanye appoints himself its high priest. In the devastating final four bars of the third verse, he dismisses the aggregate of his detractors with a lewd pun. Confidence is sexy and this is the sexiest song on the album, less a dark fantasy than a fit of magical second sight that foretells the shape of the album's true ambition.

POWER
(sic transit gloria Kanye)

At some point in the tenth or eleventh grade, virtually every high school student in America studies a unit on the great Romantic poets. Bundled in countless anthologies with Keats' "Ode to a Nightingale," Wordsworth's "Daffodils," and Byron's "She Walks in Beauty," Percy Bysshe Shelley's "Ozymandias" is one of those poems that can feel like the drably comforting wallpaper in your grandmother's upstairs bathroom – an index of the unnoticed and the overfamiliar. This is a shame, because "Ozymandias" is easily one of the weirdest, most penetrating meditations on the tragedy of human egotism ever produced. The poem:

Ozymandias
I met a traveler from an antique land
Who said: "Two vast and trunkless legs of stone
Stand in the desert.... Near them, on the sand,
Half sunk, a shattered visage lies, whose frown,
And wrinkled lip, and sneer of cold command,
Tell that its sculptor well those passions read
Which yet survive, stamped on these lifeless things,
The hand that mocked them and the heart that fed;

And on the pedestal these words appear:
My name is Ozymandias, King of Kings:
Look on my Works, ye Mighty, and despair!
Nothing beside remains. Round the decay
Of that colossal Wreck, boundless and bare
The lone and level sands stretch far away."

Nothing beside remains – in those three words floats the ancient lump in humanity's throat, the world's singular fact. Nothing lasts, life is fleeting, *sic transit gloria mundi* – thus passes the glory of the world. The poet's voice is not condescending or didactic or full of the sort of unctuousness an elder sibling might savor while ruining the Santa Claus myth for a little sister. No, the voice is numb, flattened by the awe of escaping everyday busyness long enough to fully engage the ultimate fact. You can imagine the voice narrating his encounter on a street corner to no one in particular, a man lost in the most existential sense who must remain inside the poem to survive its truth. The voice belongs equally to a grandmother on her deathbed who shares the story with a favorite grandchild, a bitterly won nugget of final wisdom to be cherished alone, later, in a private place.

That the average high school student learns "Ozymandias" as a simple moral takeaway, a souvenir to be tucked away somewhere and then forgotten, is tremendously unfortunate. More than a reflection on the triumph of entropy or the brevity of life, the poem is about how fantastically sad it is to be a human being, a creature given an ego – a miracle tool capable of devising the most intricate and ornately ambitious projects – with a built-in awareness of its own futility. Anyone who reads the poem with an eye toward having a laugh at the vanquished king's expense ("What an asshole! Boy oh boy was *he* wrong in the end!") is already a piece of that "shattered visage," an ironic accomplice to his own ignorance. We resent hubris on the level of Ozymandias' at our own peril, because his wasted empire instantiates our own lives. The poem is about power, certainly, but it is about power in a very particular way – the unique and definitively human tragedy of possessing both power (self-aware vitality) and the certainty of its demise (senescence and death). Shelley's compassion for humanity in "Ozymandias" is neither melodramatic nor insincere; it is infinite, a transcendent wind that will blow and stir the sands of our beautiful ruins forever.

If we are paying attention, we know that "Ozymandias" is always a part of contemporary life in one form or another. While in office George W. Bush unwittingly nodded to it during an interview with Bob Woodward, responding to the question of how history will view the war in Iraq. As Woodward shared with *60 Minutes* while promoting his 2007 book *Plan of Attack*: "And [Bush] said, 'History,' and then he took his hands out of his pocket[s] and kind of shrugged and extended his hands as if this is a way off. And then he said, 'History, we don't know. We'll all be dead.'" The Flaming Lips in 2002 released the song "Do You Realize??" – a pop hymn of humility and ultimate perspective amid the void, with earnest lyrics about death and human smallness – and it became one of their most widely known and beloved cuts. More recently, serialized TV masterpiece *Breaking Bad* confronted the poem head on in a July 2013 advertisement for the show's final eight episodes. A series of time-lapse shots depicting New Mexico's scarred expanse is overlaid with the voice of Bryan Cranston's meth emperor Walter White. He recites "Ozymandias" in a detached voice that passes over a slow and barely audible thud in the background, a discomfiting sound that feels like the final stone beatings of the ravaged king's heart.

It should come as no surprise, then, that *My Beautiful Dark Twisted Fantasy* – a record about the transformative decadence of a fully indulgent ego – also engages the poem's legacy, though through the prism of Kanye's narcissism. "POWER" is a twenty-first century rendition of "Ozymandias" as told from the king's point of view, at the summit of his reign. Where the speaker in Shelley's poem depended on a chance encounter with a traveler to learn the awful irony of Ozymandias, millennia after the end of his rule, we don't have to wait that long. This is the age of on-demand-everything-right-this-minute, and "POWER" is a song about Kanye's self-conscious delusion of omnipotence, a fantasy too aware of its own extravagance not to come undone. The track is a wrecking ball of egotism that, by song's end, has toppled the Ozymandias statue it just helped erect.

A brief pause here to look at Kanye's two official visual representations of "POWER" is useful, because both get at something fundamental to the music. The first comes early in his *Runaway* film. During the "Gorgeous" sequence – in which a pensive, furrowed-brow Griffin observes the phoenix lost in wonder among the menagerie of animals in his back yard – we get a snapshot of the film's symbology, with Griffin our proxy for overburdened, self-serious Kanye and the phoenix a token of his fenced-in creative purity. Hard cut to a shot of Griffin making love to an MPC2000XL machine, his fingertips massaging the chopped sample of Continent Number 6's "Afromerica" into the primitive tribal wail that pulsates throughout "POWER." The improvised hook he creates on his device casts an incantatory spell over the phoenix, who gives herself bodily to the beat, a spellbound cobra in thrall to the master's charms. The sexual self-aggrandizement here is palpable, which is precisely the point. At his finest, Kanye is hip-hop's most soulful practitioner, a shaman who communes with the samples he channels and the beats he conjures. His sonic collages have a boastful physicality, and in this scene we get to witness an erotic dramatization of his music's allure and – yes – its *power* over the listener.

The other significant visual rendering of "POWER" comes courtesy of Marco Brambilla, the renowned video collagist whose works of eschatological excess pack multiple filmed images into the space of a single frame. As reported in 2010 by Dave Itzkoff on the *New York Times* Arts Beat blog, Kanye was inspired to collaborate with Brambilla on the music video for "POWER" after seeing his installation *Civilization* hanging in the elevators of the Standard hotel in New York. A motion picture collage of looped images derived from hundreds of different films, *Civilization* reenacts Dante's *Divine Comedy* with gaudy pop referents like Arnold Schwarzenegger peopling the spaces of hell, purgatory, and heaven. Brambilla was quoted by Jori Finkel in a 2011 *Los*

Angeles Times profile describing the painterly quality of his work: "It's like I'm making a video canvas where the brushstrokes are loops or samples taken from film." Like the collaborations with Murakami and Condo on album covers, Brambilla's "POWER" video ventriloquizes the raw aesthetic drive of Kanye's music in the language of visual art. As Itzkoff describes the video: "Mr. West is seen standing imposingly with a heavy chain around his neck. As Mr. West raps, the camera slowly zooms out in one continuous, unedited take to reveal him in a classical structure, surrounded by female attendants who are partly or entirely nude; some kneel before him on all fours, others wear devil horns and still others are suspended upside down from the ceiling. The sword of Damocles hangs precariously over Mr. West's head, and behind him an unseen executioner is preparing to strike him with a blade." The video is a stunning work, a "moving painting" (as Kanye tweeted) that Brambilla described to the *Times* as "his and [Kanye]'s attempt to answer the question, 'How do you visually paint a portrait of power?'" The further out the camera slowly zooms, the more clearly we see how imperiled Kanye's Ozymandias figure is, how suffocated by decadence, how threatened by his own narcissistic illusions. Notably, the figure of Kanye – at the center of the painting, naturally – is stony, proud, unmoving.

He looks like a statue.

"POWER" opens without warning, layering the sampled hook of an obscure 1978 French disco song ("Afromerica" by Continent Number 6) to pave the way for pop music's Ozymandias. A sudden staccato eruption of clapping hands and atavistic chanting creates a sensation of worship, and as the first verse begins, Kanye locates himself in the pantheon of history – a self-proclaimed superhero for the twenty-first century – while a piercing tornado siren howls in the background. The rolling tank tread of a beat comes in at twenty-four seconds, sampling elements of funk act Cold Grits' song "It's Your Thing" (a cover of the 1969 smash hit by the Isley Brothers). A martial fury drives the song forward, Kanye's ego mobilized and on the march to wage war against...what, exactly? The easy response is to say that "POWER" was the first single from *MBDTF* and, as such, needed to be a shot across the bow, an unambiguous announcement of his return. The second verse bolsters this idea, taking aim at the cast of *Saturday Night Live* (and, by extension, the American audience) for mocking him after the Swift incident. He gives a brief account of the impulse behind his self-exile to Hawaii before delivering the song's version of Shelley's pedestal inscription, a metaphorical custody battle with Reality for his creatively unbound "inner child." This Ozymandias doesn't ask *us* to look upon his works and despair – he does it himself. The innermost contradiction that makes Kanye who he is, the one that makes him both a great artist and a great boor, is his overindulgence of everything childish within himself. The "custody" lyric evokes images of warring adults, and Kanye becomes one of them in his fight to maintain dominion over his empire of creative egotism. The implosive pressure is enormous, enough to push this Ozymandias toward thoughts of taking his own life with a sparkling handgun. The song's hook expresses profound doubts about even being Ozymandias at all and then stamps a sonic exclamation point on the whole affair with a sampled quote from the eponymous King Crimson song. The line punctuates the new Ozymandias epitaph for the digital era: "My name is Ozymandias, *21st century schizoid man*. Join me in looking upon my works and despairing."

The plagued Ozymandias of "POWER" seeks to avoid the inevitability of decay by *redefining* power. He isn't asking us to tremble at the sight of his empire, he's trying to convince us (unsuccessfully) that he doesn't care about its legacy. He tries to define power as the will to acquiesce at the moment of triumph, but no one is buying it. This is pop music's poet of narcissism, after all. A question he poses in the song's outro ("You got the power to let power go?") comes as part of a generic suicide fantasy in the outro (another ventriloquist act via collaborator Dwele) – a last-ditch effort to somehow elide the fate of all kings. The fantasy ends with the song, though, and Kanye wakes with a terrible hangover on a bed lined with softest Egyptian sheets.

All of the Lights

At one minute and two seconds, "All of the Lights (Interlude)" is the shortest track on *My Beautiful Dark Twisted Fantasy*. The first time you listen to the album from beginning to end, the unexpected instrumental feels funereal. After the adrenaline rush of "POWER" and the suicidal discharge of its ending, the interlude's melody – defined by a weight-of-the-world cello ascending from the depths of some gloomy god – feels like the release death grants the afflicted. The interlude carries within it a sadness rinsed of all impurities, an idea of grief as the known world, a perpetual winter of the soul. The Hype Williams-directed official video for "All of the Lights" – which includes the interlude as an essential preface and visual counterpoint to the song – opens on black and white images of winter in an unnamed inner city housing project. (The sequence was filmed in Rochdale Village, Queens.) The cold-open shot of a plastic board full of faceless surnames and residential unit numbers cuts to the face of an innocent young girl leaving her building. She makes her way onto a wet sidewalk lined with the kind of filthy snow you only see in large cities, snow of the dreadful hue that makes an oversensitive passerby pause to reflect on her own loneliness. Not so with the young girl on the sidewalk, though, trudging her way with sweet purpose to wherever it is she's headed. As a visual accompaniment the sequence is perfect, that rare coincidence between an artist's visualization of his music with your own imaginings. The interlude is a foreground, an approach to the record's most spectacular vista. Nothing else on *MBDTF* comes close to capturing the absolute clarity, the purity, of its vision. Like the "Let's Go Away for Awhile" instrumental on the Beach Boys' *Pet Sounds* (an album that's a plausible analogue to *MBDTF* for sheer transformative force, both in generic terms and in the evolution of its creator), the effect is ponderous. The cello's richness and yearning are impossible not to follow, and we wander with the girl through the dim geography of nightfall.

"All of the lights!" Like the alarum of a sentry warning the present about a future come too soon, the call is sounded and the song begins, exploding the interlude's protective cocoon and leaving us raw and bewildered in a place of blinding neon. A full brass section cannibalizes the interlude's melody, absorbs it and refashions it, transforming the solitude of a walk through the city at dusk into an event broadcast globally on every screen. "All of the Lights" is the grandiose central node of *MBDTF*, the singular structure that ties together a skyline full of dizzying skyscrapers. From the instant of its self-announcement, the song is a full-tilt sonic assault on the listener's capacity for wonder. An actual warning message precedes the official video – "This video has been identified by Epilepsy Action to potentially trigger

seizures for people with photosensitive epilepsy" – but it feels appropriate for the music, as well.

To grasp the significance of "All of the Lights" – to understand what it represents both for the album and for Kanye's metamorphic ego – the visual banquet of *Runaway* again proves indispensable. The sequence of the film's soundtrack corresponds roughly to the song order on *MBDTF*, and during *Runaway*'s "POWER" sequence, when the "Afromerica" sample blends with a string arrangement, the film cuts to an image of a young boy clad only in red – red shirt, red shorts, red boots – who sprints across a blighted industrial landscape at dusk. Held aloft in his right hand is a scepter that streams a wide column of bright red smoke in his wake. The piercing sound of trumpets signals a coronation, or a funeral dirge, or a warning. "All of the Lights," which scores the scene that follows, encompasses all three possibilities as a single event.

We join Griffin and the phoenix at a night parade so Felliniesque that its participants demand enumeration. We see, in no particular order, a Czech marching band clad in bright red coats, a phalanx of red-hooded Klansmen in black robes, acrobatic circus performers with sparklers, stilt-walking yin and yang angels wearing stolid bronze masks, a fusillade of pyrotechnics, and – in a weirdly moving tribute to the fallen king – a giant effigy of *Thriller*-era Michael Jackson's head, complete with red jacket. The tableau crams everything fascinating, repellent, distinctive, and wonderful about Kanye's art into a parade he throws for himself. The film cuts between shots of the spectacle and the faces of Griffin and the phoenix, the fireworks above dissolving onscreen into a pair of elementary school year-book smiles. The scene is a stunning metaphor for the entire album, an orgy of orchestrated excess that signals West's self-conscious transformation from an aspirant to the throne into the card-carrying king. "All of the Lights" is a cocktail of detonated sonic energies that, taken together, signify that transformation. From the opening lines of the first verse, there is no mistaking why we're here: "Something wrong, I hold my head / MJ gone, our nigga dead!" The specter of Michael Jackson has haunted Kanye's music since *The College Dropout*, when, on "Through the Wire," he compares his near-fatal car wreck to the hair-on-fire scare Michael had while filming a Pepsi commercial in 1984. There are MJ references in multiple songs across multiple albums. For the 2008 twenty-fifth anniversary reissue of *Thriller*, Kanye remixed "Billie Jean" (arguably Michael's signature song), slowing the tempo and adding string arrangements and a thumping backbeat. Little wonder, then, that on his first album since Michael's demise, he uses the fact of MJ's death as a personal and cultural fulcrum.

What gives the night parade in *Runaway* such ardor is the scene's saturating epiphany of redness – the way Kanye presses the *very idea* of the color red into the service of a single evocative memory: the incomparable greatness of Michael Jackson in his prime. In the annals of rock and pop music, perhaps only the color black, as a shadow land for Johnny Cash's brooding immensity, can rival MJ's world-conquering relationship to red. The red leather jackets of "Beat It" and "Thriller" were always much more than pop touchstones of a time and place, slickly overdetermined tokens of a supernatural fame. For those of us who spent childhood enthralled by his spell, red belonged to Michael as an associated fact, an extension of his mystique and the color of his greatness. Kanye nods in deference to that idea with his parade, a chromatic obsession to rival Gatsby's lust for the green luminescence.

At its core "All of the Lights" is an ironic ode to greatness and celebrity, empathetically told from the perspective of a desperate man just released from prison who scrambles to reassemble the pieces of his life. The song is unique on *MBDTF* for being a narrative that Kanye inhabits as someone else. If you detect a messianic impulse here – Christ among the lowliest of us – you're not alone. On an album so single-mindedly self-involved, a fantasy imagined through the eyes of someone *who is not* Kanye West burns with a righteous contrast. Having done time for assaulting his old lady, the first verse opens with the ex-con delivering the linchpin MJ lyric. In the absence of Michael Jackson from the world, the man finds the only metaphor big enough to distill his hope-lessness and dread. Determined to make things right in a decentered universe, he returns to his broken home with nothing but an urgency to make up for lost time. He climbs the stairs to his apartment and finds a stranger has replaced him. The pre-hook is a litany of overstimulation, lights of all sorts trapping the ex-con at every turn, setting up the freefall of the hook, the bright shiny object that ironizes the glamour of fame, recasting the visibility of celebrity as a spotlight shone from atop a prison guard tower. The idea of escape under cover of darkness is an illusion, because the lights are built into the fabric of the culture. They exist to capture and broadcast every fuckup, every stumble, every mistake. The ex-con is as much a prisoner now as ever, and his narrative is an obvious metaphor for Kanye's best laid plans, a parable of good intentions eroding in the face of his own entrenched resistance.

The moving second verse features the ex-con, against whom a restraining order is now in place, meeting up with his estranged family at a Border's Books (an unintentionally poignant reference to the now-defunct chain) for a public visitation with his daughter. He makes a searing, penitent plea to whomever will listen, and the force of his earnestness and desperation feels like Kanye breaking the fourth wall and addressing us as a collective audience. The sincerity tumbles out of his mouth ("I made mistakes, I bumped my head"), it's all he has left, and the gulf between what's happening lyrically – a lonely man dangling on the lip of the abyss – and musically – a polyvocal, multi-instrumental tsunami of *more* – swallows Kanye's ex-con in a miasma of excess. The small tale of an outcast's struggle to hustle some dignity comes wrapped in a production so awesomely decadent it would make Marie Antoinette blush, and the contrast links the song inexorably to its cultural moment, to the Great Recession and Wall Street v. Main Street. This idea is made explicit in the third verse (sung by an exquisitely strung-out-sounding Fergie), in which a benumbed voice, pushed beyond the brink by credit card debt and unemployment, straddles the void. The trance the singer falls into by the end of the verse is total – we are stranded in the echo chamber of an anonymous desiccated woman's consciousness, as far from the glittering untruth of fame as humanly possible. It is unclear what exactly she's prepared to do "this time," but whatever it is, we sense the finality of the consequences. A choir of voices sings the hook one final time before the song's outro, a soaring lamentation of powerlessness belted by Sir Elton John and Alicia Keys – "I tried to tell you but all I could say was...ohh ohh" – that leaves us alone again on a sludge-strewn city street at night.

Monster

Who or what is the monster of this song's title? Is it indie folk shaman Justin Vernon, whose macabre and distorted intro vocals snuff out the lights of the preceding track with sadistic glee? Is it the obese monstrosity Rick Ross, whose lion attack of an intro verse nearly swallows the rest of the song whole? Is it Kanye West, a swaggering and concupiscent pharaoh from the future? Is it Kanye's less artistic but more responsible big brother Jay Z, whose monstrous wealth and power as the *eminence gris* of hip-hop have made him the target of countless insatiable vampires? Surely the monster is Nicki Minaj, who – in a verse riven with dissociative identity, cannibalism, and demonic possession – delivers the most virtuosic MC performance on *My Beautiful Dark Twisted Fantasy*?

The song is the real monster here, of course, a "Monster Mash" of sorts – the first of two consecutive posse cuts in the middle of the album. The *posse cut* is a track on which four or more artists rap, and it has a long and venerable tradition in hip-hop music. Originally a viable way for an MC to garner exposure for members of his posse (by allowing them to rap on his song), the posse cut morphed over time into gatherings of already established A-list rappers eager to break bread over rhymes. A Tribe Called Quest's "Scenario" (1992) is the oft-cited exemplar of this type of collaboration. What we hear in "Monster" is a different species of four-headed creature, however. Reviewing *MBDTF* for the *Chicago Sun-Times*, critic Thomas Conner uses the metaphor of social media to distinguish Kanye's get-togethers from those of everyone else:

> *My Beautiful Dark Twisted Fantasy*. . .may be the world's first social media album. . .The overall content is guided by Kanye, the account holder, but friends and followers pop in all the time with their comments and contributions, pokes and posts. . .But these aren't guests like on every other hip-hop record, nor are they collaborations. Every sound on [the album] is a sample, a sonic fragment West uses to build his set pieces. . .Each guest's participation seems particularly purposeful, not just some babbling to fill in a blank left behind for whenever they make it by to the studio. They're not performances, they're contributions . . .

What "Monster" does better than any other track on *MBDTF* is evoke the raw thrill of the chase, the ravenous ego's blood-lusty hunt for ever more satisfying (and grotesque) forms of embodiment. Ross throws us to the lions with nothing but our wits in his boom bap intro verse. "Bitch, I'm a monster, no-good blood sucker," he foams after a bestial roar, proceeding to call himself "fat motherfucker" while chasing the listener "through the jungle" with the threat of a rumbling Kanye West sample. "Monster" is one of only two tracks on

MBDTF ("All of the Lights" is the other) that does not use an element or sample from another song. This fact adds a nice layer of connotative irony to the title, viz. in Kanye's sonic universe a song *not* constructed Frankenstein-style from the various and sundry body parts of other tracks is the real aberrant creature. The beat in "Monster" – throbbing madly in the middle distance – invokes a conspiracy of malignant forces, a rotational implement of death spinning somewhere deep within the jungle dark. The beat is a continuous threat, never veering too close, never receding too far in the background, only looming, idling, rattling around in your head as the song's bad conscience.

Kanye's verse is a strutting manic episode, opening with his deadpan claim to be the "best living or dead hands down" and proving it with lines like: "No matter who you go and get / Ain't nobody cold as this / Do the rap and the track / Triple double no assist." We hear a lascivious echo of the ruler theme from "POWER" when he asks a sexually self-congratulatory question, then – unable to restrain himself – follows it up with an even cruder punch line, a gilded misogynist over-eager to shove his ego down his subject's throat. In the next two lines he plays with that idea linguistically, punning goofily on a slang term for oral sex to conflate academic excellence with sexual entitlement. Finally, by way of a quick couplet to explain his origin, this monster returns to the jungle depths a greater enigma than when his verse began: "I'm living in the future so the present is my past / My presence is a present kiss my ass!"

Untethered as Kanye's verse is, the pathology that distinguishes "Monster" from the rest of *MBDTF* is Minaj's show-stopping contribution in the song's final verse, a frenzied psychotic dialogue between her two alter egos (Roman Zolanski and Barbie) that threatens to hijack the entire album. The only recent scene-stealing performance of this caliber was Kendrick Lamar's assaultive turn on Big Sean's 2013 song "Control," a verse that set fire to moribund hip-hop blogs the world over. Minaj subs her alter egos in and out of the verse with the recklessness of a baseball coach on acid, and the result is a hostage situation that happens in the basement of the song's grindhouse. The Jake Nava-directed video attempts to do justice to Minaj's virtuosity, depicting the pink-haired Barbie alter ego bound in a chair and tortured by Roman's S&M vampire, black gothic lace and leather in a life-or-death struggle with white tulle. The verse is too combustible for any single representation, though, and the more you listen to it, the more dumbfounded you become that it doesn't eviscerate everything else on the record. Has any verse in a pop song of the past twenty years so perversely affirmed Whitman's ultra-American maxim "I contain multitudes"? Minaj's monster is too far gone to worry about questions of feminism, though she exhorts us to "watch the queen conquer" while she collects "50K for a verse" without an album to her name. Whatever she is, we think to ourselves, she isn't human. What she accomplishes in a few bars is too vicious and unforgiving to be human.

"Monster" gambols into the exhilaration and terror of an ego gaining self-awareness, a paean to what it feels like to activate the potential energies lodged within pure confidence. The result is a schizophrenic horror show, and one of the strongest tracks on the album.

So Appalled

The British prog rock outfit Manfred Mann's Earth Band (MMEB) reached the top of the Billboard Hot 100 in February of 1977 – four months before Kanye West was born in Atlanta – with a cover of Bruce Springsteen's "Blinded by the Light." It's the version of the song you know best, most likely, the one you can hear today on any ecumenical commercial FM station lumping pop songs from 1960 to 1999 under the generically depressing aegis of "oldies." The cover's organ and overpowering Moog synth lend the MMEB version a certain narcotic urgency, a windblown scent of seventies spiritual desperation, that you won't find on Springsteen's cut. Part of the song's legacy is the confusion it spawned by changing some of the lyrics from the original chorus. Springsteen's "cut loose like a Deuce" became "revved up like a Deuce," and the slurred sibilance of MMEB's lead singer prompted legions of pre-Internet listeners to mishear the line as "wrapped up like a douche" and waste precious moments of their lives debating the possibility.

Thirty-three years later pop music's best known douche was in the studio channeling MMEB, sampling the bridge from the band's translucent, lovely oddity "You Are – I Am" for "So Appalled," the seventh cut on *My Beautiful Dark Twisted Fantasy*. The sample is soaked in the revelatory paranoia of a sci-fi thriller's denouement, and a feeling of sustained dread becomes the song's condition of possibility. Producer and sometime rapper Swizz Beatz delivers the intro, an agonized parody of a hip-hop cliché that sounds, by design, "ridiculous." The effect is a pronounced cognitive dissonance between the intro's lyrical content and its sonic enfoldment – between the hype-heavy signifiers of a traditional Top 40 hip-hop song ("Throw your hands in the air, if you's a true player!") and the doomy hellstorm happening just outside your window. The nuclear fallout atmospherics of "So Appalled" are heavy with thickness and haze, the beat full of trepidation, and we lurch forward with the spastic wariness of a child in a haunted house (the song's doom-eagerness made it the obvious choice to follow "Monster" on the album). The soundscape evokes a sense of movement through peril – a strategic escape from a burning building, perhaps, or a one-breath-at-a-time trek through a combat zone.

"So Appalled," like "Monster," is a posse cut, with five different artists (in addition to Kanye) providing a verse, hook, or bridge. Lyrically speaking, the track is the weakest on *MBDTF*. Each verse is a semi-ironic ode to the opulence made possible by success, but none has the compressed ferocity or single-minded delirium of the verses on "Monster." What makes the song exceptional is its temperamental friction, its utterly original deconstruction of tired hip-hop tropes through a prism of fear and trembling. Kanye raps his verse in a subtly altered register and sounds like a completely different person, a self-styled stranger in a land he's deter-mined to defamiliarize. In his verse Jay Z parses the contra-diction in hip-hop's heart, paraphrasing Aaron Eckhart's Harvey Dent character in the bleak 2008 Batman sequel *The Dark Knight* ("You either die a hero, or live long enough to see yourself become the villain"). We rarely get this kind of candor – disgust at the zero sum game of popularity and authenticity – from a major league hip-hop artist. "So Appalled" would be the easy standout track on countless hip-hop records, but on *MBDTF* it merely fascinates, convection waves rising from the scorched earth.

Devil in a New Dress

The magic hour is that bleeding gash in time just before sunset, that nether part of the day when a heartbreaking light limns the horizon with color, and the sky seems to absorb and refract the world's most sorrowful possibilities. Day cedes its dominion to night as shadows lengthen past the point of maximal distortion, severing their ties with the realm of rational objects. A kind of opaque fluid washes over the edges of our awareness. Mystery rather than clarity becomes the governing principle. This is a place of hybrid convergence, a literal twilight zone, where the world's irrational forces are poised to overtake the natural order, or – worse still – reveal themselves to be the most essential part of what we thought we knew.

"Devil in a New Dress" opens with a glint of sound, a falsetto voice hitting a high note of ecstasy. The voice sounds like dying light, like starlight cutting through coldest space across incalculable distance. The magic hour is upon us, and the sensation is one of floating. The falsetto belongs to Smokey Robinson, a sample of his 1973 quiet storm transformation of "Will You Love Me Tomorrow?", originally made famous by girl group the Shirelles in 1960. As pop songs from the Brill Building era go, "Will You Love Me Tomorrow?" is needier, more insecure than many of its peers. A tragic awareness haunts the lyrics, and in the Shirelles' version of the song we hear a child's first apprehension that everything – people, civilizations, romances – is bound by finitude. Smokey's cover arrived thirteen years later, all sexual atmospherics and soulful *savoir faire*. His song is sung for mature audiences, consenting adults who understand impermanence all too well but are too turned on to care about it right now. The earnest doubt of the Shirelles has been replaced by a languorous seduction. The song's basic question, as posed by Smokey, is emptied of its original content, warped into an ornament of sensitivity worn to close the deal with his lover. "Will You Love Me Tomorrow?"'s genealogy is a palimpsest that foregrounds the simmering fantasy of "Devil in a New Dress," with the former's title an unspoken rhetorical question the latter attempts to answer.

Returning to the magic hour and the timeless moment of "Devil in a New Dress," what image does the sound conjure? The song's glittering arrangement is, to my ears, a Benz convertible moving steadily into twilight, an enormous desert sky swallowing the landscape. Kanye is behind the wheel and in the passenger seat sits the Devil herself in haute couture. The couple are on what will be their final date, and Kanye is wistful, even playful, about the demise of their union. "Put your hands to the constellations / The way you look should be a sin, you my sinsation," he implores ironically in the hook, knowing she's in no mood. The evening is an echo of another ride-with-the-devil fantasy, the unimpeachably sexy 2007 "Flashing Lights" video he co-directed with Spike Jonze. In that version of events (a three-minute continuous shot) – also occurring in the magic hour – his final date with the Devil is a grim joke. She is the one driving in the desert at dusk, and he is nowhere to be seen. After stopping to get out and strip down to lingerie, she lights her clothes on fire and struts back to the car in her stilettos, the lights of Las Vegas twinkling in the distance. When she opens the trunk, we see a bound and gagged Kanye in a tux looking up with bulging, terrified eyes. Tenderly caressing his face, she reaches to pull out a shovel. The camera recedes in slow motion as she plunges its tip repeatedly into his body.

The terms of the fantasy for "Devil in a New Dress" are different, though, more ambiguous and mature. In place of an erotic death wish, this break-up is a waltz full of dreamy elegance. Time is malleable in the magic hour, subject to the systolic and diastolic rhythms of memory and deformed scraps of dream. The song transpires in both the past and present. At times Kanye speaks directly to the Devil and she is physically present beside him; at other times she is part of the past, a spectral blur he still addresses in his mind. The couple's car ride is one of those masochistic exercises in mutual defiance familiar to anyone who has ever been in a doomed relationship. Both parties are full of loathing – for each other and for themselves – and both operate from a place of maximum pettiness, each knowing that the very act of going through with the date is a surefire way to inflict discomfort on the other. Kanye acknowledges this with the song's first words, declaring "I love it though / I love it though, you know?" Doing his best to sublimate the bitterness, he tries to engage the Devil with some levity, addressing her in both the second and third person within the same verse, as though, in the midst of reminiscing with her in the car, he is suddenly somewhere else telling the story before an audience who don't laugh at what, to them, isn't supposed to be funny. The effect brings to mind the bizarre jump-cuts in dreams wherein the dreamer's conversation with a familiar acquaintance continues, uninterrupted, in spite of the acquaintance's total physical transformation into someone else. Frustrated, Kanye gets more aggressive with the Devil in a half-mocking singsong voice, and the magic hour's uncanny mutational power takes over: "Haven't said a word, haven't said a word to me this eeeevening," he needles her, echoing the looped refrain from the Smokey Robinson sample – "Tonight with words unspoken / Don't have to say a word to me, Baaaaby," Smokey intones in his lovely falsetto. The magic hour melds the two versions into something unnatural, inserting a sardonic complaint into a generous moment of tenderness shared between lovers. Satisfied with that perversion and willing to cut his losses, Kanye speeds off alone into the night, leaving the Devil by the side of the road to recede in the distance. A regretful electric guitar riff signifies the jagged break, and Rick Ross is left to clean up any loose ends in one pitiless final verse.

Runaway

To understand the song, to gain some rough sense of its place in the transhistorical pop republic, you could do worse than begin with a *Charlotte Observer* article from April 11, 2012. The piece is a local interest story and profile in miniature of Paul "Mickey" Walker and the Backyard Heavies, the Charlotte band for which Walker played drums in the early seventies. "They had a single coming out [in 1971] called 'Soul Junction,' and they needed something for the flip side," writes the *Observer*'s Tommy Tomlinson. "They came up with an instrumental based on a piano groove and a drum lick that Walker calls 'a funky march.' They called it 'Expo 83.'" Thirty-nine years later, the band had long since gone their separate ways. Walker was a social worker dedicated to helping the mentally ill homeless population in Charlotte. He received a phone call from his old band mate Roger Branch in September of 2010. Branch had been in communication with an attorney representing Def Jam Records. A famous rapper, Branch told Walker, had sampled a drum loop from "Expo 83" in a song. Walker was unclear as to who the rapper was, "texting his wife that his drum lick had been sampled by some guy named Kenya." The story ends on an optimistic note, with the three surviving members of the band receiving modest royalties from the revival of their old B-side, even making plans to record new material.

As an old-fashioned hymn of resurrection – that is one way to listen to "Runaway."

Imagine yourself standing onstage at a concert in Long Beach in July 1981. You are performing before thousands of people, and the river of narcotics in your system has breached the synaptic levies. This shit is *gorgeous*, you think to yourself, aroused in a holy moment of contemplating how sexy you must look from out there in the crowd. You are in the middle of singing "Mary Jane," one of the best songs from your debut album three years earlier, and while bantering with the audience you suddenly feel so good that you have to discharge some of the surplus energy before it evaporates your brain. "Look at ya!" you exclaim, parsing the ineffable high of being you into a throwaway of boisterous inclusion. You're Rick James, bitch, the funkiest motherfucker on the planet, and though in twenty-three years you'll be dead, tonight there is only you and this audience and the fleeting spontaneity of a joyful noise to hold it all together. Twenty-nine years later the moment is excised and transplanted in stereo into the heartbeat of the twenty-first century's most ambitious pop song. Severed from the bonds of time, that happy exclamation – Look at ya! – is a specter that haunts its new home. No longer the sound of a cup running over, it has become an accusation. Whatever hermetically sealed sense of connection and transaction the outburst once contained is gone. What is left is an ice pick of self-disgust.

Another way to listen to "Runaway" – as the atrophy of context.

Forget Walker's drum lick. Time is the funky march, the syncopated breakbeat played back to you at odd tempos by your memory. Time samples your life, compresses and extends and loops whole chunks of it. Time can amplify the overtones of a long gone lover's sigh, rewrite the lyrics to your marriage vows. Manipulating the shape of our experience, time heals our wounds by changing the way we remember them. The site of today's demoralizing collapse is the groundbreaking for tomorrow's greatest triumph.

Kanye understands this principle, experiments with it. His best samples play with the idea of time's weirdness, its transformative irony, discovering the sonic vernacular of the future in the scattered potsherds of the past. Those who complain his songs are recycled pop throwaways are, in a manner of speaking, correct. The drum sample from "Expo 83," for example, forms the chassis of "Runaway," but it does so once removed, subsumed within another sample, the breakbeat intro to "The Basement" from Pete Rock and CL Smooth's 1992 debut LP *Mecca and the Soul Brother*. Time enfolds upon itself in the beat, 2010 via 1992 by way of 1971. Three separate histories are compressed into a single sonic pulse, yet this nested interdependence fosters the creation of a unique living thing, something far greater than its parts.

The pop persona in "Runaway" is heir to an amalgam of ego gestures and bravura performances stretching back at least as far as 1968, the year of Elvis Presley's televised comeback special, and – recall – narcissism's breakthrough into the psychiatric mainstream. Thanks to YouTube, the video repository for global collective memory, a quick search yields multiple edited versions of the special. Watching it with the knowledge that nearly half a century has passed since its recording, one seeks in vain to account for the force of the performance. In *Mystery Train*, his classic of American cultural criticism, Greil Marcus cites the comeback special as a high point of Elvis's engagement with his own ego: "It was the finest music of his life. If ever there was music that bleeds, this was it. Nothing came easy that night, and he gave everything he had – more than anyone knew was there."

A deity bedecked in black leather insouciance, Comeback Special Elvis understands the audience's collective stake in his mythos. His performance is a generous egomania that, rather than viewing the world as a mirror, reflects the culture's most vital and inchoate fantasies back to it as a flesh-and-blood *fait accompli*. There is a brief moment during the special, between song sets, when Elvis, sitting in a small circle with his band members and reminiscing about the world he created, has a laugh at his own expense. "Now wait a minute, wait a minute, something's wrong with my lip," he mumbles, a reference to his signature facial gesture. He fumbles with his upper lip. "You remember that, don't you?" he asks, raising it in the old, archetypal way, awash in the contingent silliness of history. "I've got news for you, baby. I did twenty-nine pictures like that." The audience laughs and applauds with a reverential awe, and we understand this is not so much a comeback special as it is a revival. The ego on display is something regenerative and communal, a sublimated social wish to play fast and loose with unlimited freedom. Elvis turns a trademark into a throwaway for the sake of a laugh, and we realize the potency that a supreme American pop figure has – that it takes an Elvis to efface an Elvis, even if only for a moment.

In his eponymous hagiography of "Like a Rolling Stone," Marcus describes the song's opening sound – a drumstick's rifle report on the surface of a snare – as an "absolute announcement" of something new. "Then for an expanding instant there is nothing," he writes. "The first sound is so stark and surprising, every time you hear it, that the empty split-second that follows calls up the image of a house tumbling over a cliff; it calls up a void." "Runaway" is a descendant of "Like a Rolling Stone," a kaleidoscopic epic constructed with an equally keen sense of egotistic precision. Both songs are caustic valedictions. Dylan bids a fond and annihilating farewell to an ex-love amid the scene of her crumbling false ideals; Kanye pushes his lover out the door with an emotionally shambolic full-on confession of his failings. "Runaway" is an inversion of its forebear's world-straddling bravado, however. Where Dylan's ironic fairy tale expands and ascends with a gleeful contempt, a complete satisfaction that submerges the world beneath a flood of riotous final judgment, "Runaway" tunnels inward to the diamond-encrusted core of West's self-pity. "Like a Rolling Stone" is the sound of an expanding universe; "Runaway" is the singularity of narcissism's black hole. If we hear an echo of forgiveness in the boundless, timeless joy of Dylan's "total song," we feel, listening to Kanye's, the frostbite of self-contempt.

"Runaway" opens with its own starkness, a single repeated note of lonely insistence. An E key sounds fifteen staccato times on a piano. The immediate feeling is one of real threat, a foreboding that the lonely E will be the only sound you will ever hear again until, mercifully, a transitional lower E is struck, followed by three D sharps. The progression is a descent, a numb walk down the soul's Weimar staircase. "That which God is to use He first reduces to nothing," Kierkegaard writes, and that idea is given flesh in these opening moments – an absolute reduction is precisely what we hear. In an album overflowing with fantastical embellishments of every sort, there is real pathos in the choice to open a song this ambitious with a single repetitive note. Once at the bottom of the staircase, in the serene darkness of a large room, the beat enters and it's like someone turns on the lights. The ghostly Rick James *Look at ya!* encircles the room from above, both an ambush and a vulture. The effect is reminiscent of the cartoonish trope in eighties sitcoms, wherein a child's bad conscience is depicted as the floating head of a disapproving adult. Your eyes adjust to the light and you see that the room is a banquet hall with row upon row of white linen tables and seated guests. The guests are silent, though their faces familiar. As your mind catches up to cognitively make sense of what you're looking at, you have an awful realization: The faces belong to all the people you've ever wronged, hell's version of *This Is Your Life*, collected here in one place to crush you with the weight of their aggregated judgment. Outmatched and outnumbered, wholly vulnerable, you do the one thing you never did in your dealings with them. You tell the truth. You own up to how destructive your solipsism has been, how toxic to everyone else. Uncharacteristically, the admission does not arrive couched in evasive gestures or grandiose rationalization. Some of the guests' heads start to nod in recognition at the sound of your honesty. You *do* find fault in everything, they think to themselves. We *have* tolerated your behavior beyond reasonable limits. Your voice is a plea. An odd humility diffuses throughout the banquet hall, and the guests can tell that you mean it. To truly acquit yourself, however, you know that you need more than remorse. You need a grand ironic gesture, a demonstration that – though no lesson has been learned, no moral imparted – you are, in your ambivalent way, sorry. You package your basic contradiction into the shape of an apology that is not an apology, a champagne toast not to all these people you've disappointed, but – unbelievably – to your own shortcomings. You use the words "douchebags," "assholes," and "jerkoffs" in your toast, plurals all, as if your grandiosity will not allow you to seek a reprieve for yourself alone, but for the very idea of the overstepping narcissist as a type of human being.

The kicker, the part that no one except you could have predicted? They forgive you.

The final three minutes and six seconds of "Runaway" are what drive it beyond the outskirts of a potentially radio-friendly pop town and into the lawless hill country of art. The final third of the song – a wrenching and distorted recapitulation of the previous six minutes as filtered through a vocoder – alienates anyone who expects not to be alienated. As so many critics and fans noted upon hearing it for the first time, the final part of "Runaway" should in no way succeed. It is overlong and confusing and frankly unnecessary as a coda to an already stunning pop masterpiece. Attempted by just about any other major artist, the same three minutes and six seconds would likely generate a week-long meme fest mocking it on Twitter and then fall promptly into oblivion. Yet it does work. It works so well that, without it, the song's entire emotional economy would be systemically flawed; the value we extract from the first two-thirds would be the worthless currency of a failed state. The vocoder part of "Runaway" is analogous to a definitive life choice, the kind that indicates unambiguously to the world exactly who you have decided to be. As it drones anxiously over an exquisite string arrangement: It sounds like a suicidal android at open mic night. It sounds like a pilot reading the beatitudes through a broken intercom to the passengers of a doomed flight. It sounds like a dial-up connection confessing its love to a pay phone. It sounds like a warning message from the near future sent by a race of bodiless digital posthumans. It sounds like the feeling of having something vitally important to say and not having language to say it. It sounds like a hangover swearing off alcohol. It sounds like a long-in-the-tooth iPad lecturing a class of drones on empathy. It sounds like the failure of logic in a moment of distilled emotion. It sounds like a lonely person's digitally scrambled sense of himself in a culture of total connectedness.

During the banquet scene in *Runaway*, a discontent Griffin gets up from the table and walks across the room to an ancient white piano. He pauses and, with the calculated impatience of a stubborn toddler, bangs his finger on a lonely out-of-tune E key twelve times. A second or so of silence persists between each note. With the sounding of that first haggard note, we become captives within the conflicted heart of who Kanye West is. As his finger repeats the note with a kind of despairing force and we find ourselves staring into another void, something remarkable happens. A flying "V" of ballerinas in black leotards comes rushing across the concrete warehouse floor to accompany Griffin and his white piano. An androgynous blond-bobbed prima ballerina quietly sidles up to the piano, extends her leg high above her head, and the performance begins. Kanye stands behind the weathered instrument crooning in his cream-colored tuxedo jacket with rounded black lapels and black bow tie, the ballet before him a choreographed expression of his basic conflict. The scene is full of an exotic heartbreak, each self-sufficient movement of each ballerina a gesture of opacity, a rendering in flesh of unknowable human motivation. Why does Kanye West act the way he does?

The Condo album cover painting of a startled, doe-eyed ingénue with a handlebar mustache wearing a black tutu, a glass of red wine in her delicately extended hand, contributes to the iconic association of the ballerina with the song. Condo's ballerina is toasting, of course. "Runaway," we are to understand, is a work of art as fully choreographed as a ballet. Its place on a pop music album is almost incidental to its aspiration for self-transcendence. This is because art does more than imitate life for Kanye West. Listening to "Runaway," wholly engrossed in its nine minute apologetic of the self, we learn that art justifies Kanye's excesses. It gives sublime context to the consequences of his worst mistakes, translates his inscrutable motives into boldly comprehensible language. Incorporating the raw material of his necrotic emotional tissue, art performs miracles of healing that no amount of public apologies, press junkets, stints in treatment centers, therapy sessions with Oprah, or trips to Paris could ever achieve. That look of astonishment on the face of Condo's ballerina captures the experience of hearing this song for the very first time, and every time thereafter.

Hell of a Life

The first throbbing fifteen seconds of distorted bass signify the mind of someone premeditating his own depravity. The sound is the feeling of arousal, biological on the level of instinct, the rush of quickening blood flow as heard from deep within a human skull. "Hell of a Life" begins its sonic binge with a dragged-through-molasses sampling of "She's My Baby," a juke joint blues-inspired song from 1966 by minor San Francisco psychedelics the Mojo Men. In this fantasy Kanye has eschewed the glamorous and ironic posturing of "Runaway" for a life less contorted. There will be no more kowtowing to the wide offended world. He has taken his own advice, flooring his Lamborghini at top speed away from the social acceptance he flirted with in "Runaway."

Though every track on *MBDTF* guides the listener down a glittering corridor in the service of one ego need or another, this is Kanye at his most lascivious, his most reductively libidinal. (Only *Yeezus*' debauched romp "I'm in It" is more licentious.) Where "Devil in a New Dress" moves at the leisurely pace of a fop in his garden, taking its time to savor the blurred ironies of the magic hour, "Hell of a Life" rushes headlong into Kanye's pornographic lost weekend with both feet bound to the pedal. The song is impatient to court your disgust, and the first line – "I think I just fell in love with a porn star" – is tame by comparison with what follows. The first verse goes to extraordinary comic extremes in the interest of representing the fantasy's power – a nun reaches spontaneous orgasm, a priest faints, an elderly man develops an ulcer from desire. The porn star of this song is the patron saint of sexual excess, a pornographic rendering of Too Much made flesh and blood and thong. This saint has blessed/cursed Kanye with egoistic powers beyond human understanding; by the end of the first verse he's levitating and taunting the Devil, delaying the eventual moment that hell will consume him.

The song's hook samples one of the most beloved riffs in all rock and roll, the introduction to Black Sabbath's "Iron Man." In recent years the riff has achieved mainstream currency again with the release of the *Iron Man* films, though as anyone conversant with Sabbath will tell you, the song was written by band member Geezer Butler about a time traveling witness to a future apocalypse who, upon returning to the present, is transformed by a magnetic field into a lumbering and inelegant steel golem. Mute and thus unable to warn us about what's coming, contemporary society finds him an odd amusement and has fun at his expense. This enrages the iron man and he has his vengeance by destroying civilization, thus serving as the catalyst of the horror he witnessed in the future. The story is one of the tried and true tropes of science fiction, a classic causal loop whereby the would-be agent of change is predestined to set in motion the series of events that produce the undesirable outcome. The song's original working title was "Iron Bloke," which – thankfully for the sake of the riff's immortal cool – was not the preordained final result.

As sampled in "Hell of a Life," the interpolated riff buoys the hook, whose lyrics indicate Kanye deflects the disapproval of an enfeebled superego by doubling down on his fantasy, convinced his depravity can sustain the fantasy. We hear an echo of the "Iron Man" lyrics in that first line with the question of whether sanity has fled, only now it's interiorized, the outside world's collective voice of reason as ventriloquized by Kanye to himself. He is punch drunk with the pornography of excess. "Pussy and religion" are effectively identical, the only reasons to live in the world of the song's fantasy. The hook's final entreaty is addressed to the professionally erotic muse, Saint Too Much, and it puns morbidly on the phrase "hell of a life," signifying both the illusion of an eternally titillating debauch and the ineluctable reality of escapism's abyss.

Late in the second verse, in a free associative cascade of rhyming images, Kanye has another intrusive moment of foreboding. Commenting on the weird economics of a porn star's repertoire (viz. that anal sex and group sex, or "gang bang," fetch about the same price on the market), he launches into a twisted syllogism that equates group sex, gang brutality, slavery, and death by gunfire with the emotional hell of coming down from his fantasy. The sound of his "bang, bang, bang, bang" is flaccid and depressive, a subtle nod to the truth that the Lamborghini will one day run out of gas. By the third verse Kanye is all in, though, pushing the fantasy's logical extension past its breaking point. Wanting to have it all, both the fantasy of asocial decadence and the more realistic American version with a yard and a baby, he imagines what married life to the porn star might look like. The obvious joke to be made here about an open marriage is not too obvious for Kanye, who has a laugh at the idea of both husband *and* wife sleeping with the bridesmaids. Life will be an endless succession of role-playing sex, he imagines, sex so devastatingly great that it sidelines him for whole days at a time. He wonders which Oscar party they'll attend together as a couple, ponders what she might wear when they step out in the world with nothing to hide from anyone. During a flash of tenderness and compassion, he even imagines an Oscar de la Renta employee publicly shaming his wife for trying on a dress in the store. He imagines scolding the judgmental employee with a rhetorical question that doubles as a question posed to the world judging him, his own version of Christ's "plank in your own eye" comment in the Sermon on the Mount. Finally, by the song's outro, the compressed fantasy finally walks out of the strip club and into the nervous light of Sunday morning. Kanye is recounting to himself the events of the night, compressing the fantasy into a set of three hilariously digestible images – a marriage in a bathroom, a dance floor honeymoon, and a quickie divorce later the same night. The party is over.

Why is this song stationed on the record between "Runaway" – the soaring and triumphal "backhanded apology" for the contradiction of Kanye's persona – and "Blame Game" – a trek into his own emotional Chernobyl? "Hell of a Life" operates like the bridge between two distinct states of feeling, the only way to get from one to the other. Picking up exactly where "Runaway" ends, gathering the loose threads of sonic distortion, "Hell of a Life" gives them shape and form. Both on the run *from* and *toward* the day of his emotional reckoning, he overdoses on sexual excess, using the fantasy to escape as far within himself as possible. The specter of Sabbath's mute iron bloke, encased within an impenetrable shell and dying to be understood, never trails too far behind in this song, one that finds West so deeply and narcissistically ensconced within his own indulgent fantasy that it takes the harrowing annihilation of "Blame Game" to extract him.

Blame Game

The wrenching melody we hear in "Blame Game," the most painful cut on *My Beautiful Dark Twisted Fantasy*, comes via a sample of electronic musician Aphex Twin's elegiac "Avril 14th." A piano composition just under two minutes long, "Avril 14th" is a glimmer of unnamable sadness, a whispered idea that seeps into the soul's cracks and quietly drowns the listener from within. Exquisitely spare, beautiful in the way of Siberian sunsets, the song is all pressurized heartache, a grief burst struggling to escape. The piano melody ambles through the two minutes in a sublime daze, a newly minted widower shuffling through the hallways of his house. "Avril 14th" carries within it that most insidious type of sadness, the kind so world-altering – so annihilatingly complete – that its awed victim comes to associate it with beauty. Any trauma or tragedy that could precipitate a melody this haunting is somehow aligned with final things, we sense, somehow in league with death.

"Blame Game" translates the utter psychological degradation of a failed relationship into a pop record. Opening with a heavy sigh and the sampled piano melody from "Avril 14th," we are immediately in a cordoned-off zone of emotional crisis, a triage center of the mind where Kanye's splintered ego works to piece together a series of unhappy facts into a tolerable perspective. Pushing the song forward beyond its own sickly-sweet inertia is a percussion sample, the whispering drumroll and understated beat from J. J. Johnson's "Parade Strut" – an instrumental off the official soundtrack of 1974 blaxploitation film *Willie Dynamite*. Guest R&B singer John Legend lends the smooth dignity of his voice to the hook, an ironic lyrical entreaty addressed to the song's estranged lover. The "blame game" is a masochistic blood sport, and the singer is addicted to playing. The first verse finds Kanye scribbling a quasi-romantic cliché ("I'd rather argue with you than be with someone else") on a bathroom wall, then immediately negating it by finding someone else to take home. At 2 a.m. his will breaks, however. He calls his lost love and hangs up before she can answer, and the soul's dark night plays tricks on him, as is its wont. He begins to blame himself for the way things ended and he cries out for help. John Legend flies into the room to rock him to sleep, the heart-rending hook a sudden lullaby for the terminally grief-stricken.

A whiff of desperation, of bargaining, taints the start of the second verse, with Kanye promising new levels of intimacy to his lost love if she'll stick things out a while longer and see what happens. He gets sentimental about how much time has passed since they had rough sex in public, and it's at that thought of sex – the realization that she is now having it with other men who are not Kanye West – when "Blame Game" takes a breathtaking schizoaffective turn toward conceptual art. With manipulated vocals that sonically enact the psychosis of a scorned lover and embody his faltering capacity to think clearly – a mind clouded with rationalizations, shards of memory, second-guesses, and recriminations – Kanye falls apart before our very ears, losing even his sense of where he is in the album when he briefly begins singing the hook of "All of the Lights" in a vocoderized aside. The voices claw into the song's interior space like demons eager to ransack an altar. Some of the voices are high-pitched and thin, stretched across a Procrustean bed of self-loathing. Some are dense and massive, rising from below to swallow any thought not wholly dedicated to vengeance and rage. Coming from every direction, these voices assail and suffocate Kanye, overwhelming him with their relentlessness. When the hook finally arrives we wonder if there is enough of him left to finish the song.

For the third verse he recites part of a prose poem ("Your Bitter is My Sweet") by Chloe Mitchell, the self-proclaimed "Basquiat of Poetry" Kanye commissioned to write something specifically for "Blame Game." The poem is a thematic restatement of the song, a riff on that saddest of emotional mysteries whereby the love between two people – once an indestructible organism of fearless intensity – can double back on itself in the form of an all-consuming hatred. We hear the words and realize it's been there all along, the idea of erasure and annihilation, in the sparkling austerity of the "Avril 14th" sample. We recognize "Blame Game" as an answer song willing to tell the Shirelles the truth fifty years too late, to respond to the pleading question at the heart of "Will You Love Me Tomorrow?" with a tone so final, so devastating, that not only their question but the very idea of their *needing to ask* seems silly and absurd. The song's brief second hook, which precedes the fourth verse, is the evisceration that accompanies letting go. John Legend has left the building and Kanye is all alone. He sings the hook "I can't love you this much" twice for good measure – and it functions as a kind of catharsis, freeing him to finish the job of officiating this funeral.

At seven minutes and forty-nine seconds, "Blame Game" is second only to "Runaway" for the title of longest track on *MBDTF*. And, as in "Runaway," the final third of the song is a brash experiment pitting style against substance. Where "Runaway" ends with a three-minute vocoderized soliloquy reenacting the song's drama as distortion, "Blame Game" ends with "The Best Birthday Ever," a skit featuring the overheard conversation between Chris Rock – who plays the fictional new fling of Kanye's lost love – and the gone girl herself. As a blood-and-guts portrayal of unremitting bitterness, it is only fitting that the song's fourth and final verse leads into what happens next. Kanye understands that his lost love is out there somewhere living her life; it could not be otherwise. He is coming to terms with that fact, steering his mind in the direction of acceptance, though he's not quite there and still obeys a compulsion to call her. The phone rings and rings and she does not answer. Introduced through the clever conceit of her phone accidentally butt-dialing him back, we listen along with him ("And I heard the whole thing") as the scene unfolds on the other end of the line: Chris Rock's lothario is effusively praising his lover postcoitus for her newly evolved sexual dynamism. It's his birthday, and in addition to a watch he had been coveting, his girl has given him the most life-affirming sex of his life. His disbelief is palpable, and he seeks ever cruder and more hilarious ways to express his awe at how far she's come. Her reply to each of his obsequious rhetorical questions? "Yeezy taught me."

For some, the skit is comic relief to offset the song's harrowing first five minutes. Having just plumbed the depths of Yeezy's disintegrated consciousness and borne witness to the oozing sores of his regret, who among us doesn't need a laugh? Yet the skit is also a play on the irrational male horror of feminine sexuality. In Barry Hannah's eternal short story "Water Liars," the narrator struggles to accept his wife's admission of having a sexual past that predates their own:

> My sense of the past is vivid and slow. I hear every sign and see every shadow. The movement of every limb in every passionate event occupies my mind. I have a prurience on the grand scale. It makes no sense that I should be angry about happenings before she and I ever saw each other. Yet I feel an impotent homicidal rage in the matter of her lovers. She has excused my episodes as the course of things, though she has a vivid memory too. But there is a blurred nostalgia men have that women don't.
>
> You could not believe how handsome and delicate my wife is naked.
>
> I was driven wild by the bodies that had trespassed her twelve and thirteen years ago.

The decision to conclude "Blame Game" with the gory details of such an explicit encounter, the choice to reimagine it with such masochistic zeal, belongs to the same species of self-destructive horror that plagues Hannah's narrator. Just as the vocoder outro is integral to the emotional superstructure of "Runaway," "Blame Game" would fail to cross the finish line without "The Best Birthday Ever" bringing up the rear, as it were. We laugh because Rock's performance is full of his signature abrasive generosity. His character in the skit is dumbstruck with gratitude for inheriting so many wonderful things from the death of Kanye's relationship. He sees himself simply as the winner in a zero sum game, someone tickled by his own good fortune. He is so bowled over by the benefits accruing to him as a result of Yeezy's loss that he vows to seek Kanye out and thank him. He promises to buy *MBDTF* in multiple formats. The voice of his lover is nasal and harsh; she sounds like a fembot from a caricatured Long Island. Yet the whole thing is suddenly unfunny when imagined from Kanye's vantage point, his trembling hand working to keep the phone steady enough at his ear for him to hear clearly, unable to hang up on the nightmare unfolding at the other end of the line.

He distracts us with lowbrow, offensive comedy while demanding our empathy, a contradiction that – you could reasonably argue – is what makes him the artist he is.

Lost in the World

"The rumors are true. And then some," critic Ryan Dombal blogged in a Pitchfork post from August 13, 2010. "Bon Iver mastermind Justin Vernon laid vocals down on 'at least 10 songs' during three separate week-long trips to record with Kanye West in Hawaii earlier this year." Three months later Dombal would earn a very specific form of celebrity among Pitchfork readers when he gave *My Beautiful Dark Twisted Fantasy* a perfect 10.0 rating – the fabled and elusive breakdancing unicorn of online music criticism. Dombal's blog post features an interview with Vernon, who distills the surreality of his experience working on the album thusly: "That whole first week I was there we worked on the 'Woods' song, which is called 'Lost in the World'. We were just eating breakfast and listening to the song on the speakers and [Kanye]'s like, 'Fuck, this is going to be the festival closer.' I was like, 'Yeah, cool.' It kind of freaked me out."

It's an image that makes you smile by virtue of its seeming unlikelihood. Sitting at a breakfast table overlooking the Pacific somewhere in America's most paradisiacal environs, the world's biggest pop star talks shop over huevos rancheros with one of indie music's most distinct voices. That first blush of improbability quickly vanishes, of course. We know that the arc of Kanye's musical ethos is long and bends continually toward art, regardless of where he finds it. The backstory surrounding the critical role Vernon played in the creation of *MBDTF* has passed into the stuff of millennial music nerd lore, a Venn diagram space shared by thick beards and thicker gold chains. The indie rock darling renowned as the creative impetus behind Bon Iver's self-released 2007 debut *For Emma, Forever Ago*, Vernon's best songs are lonesome winterscapes of asphyxiating clarity. *For Emma's* conception has become a burnished indie talisman "nearly eclipsed by its own (endlessly repeated) mythology," as critic Amanda Petrusich wrote reviewing Bon Iver's 2009 EP *Blood Bank*. Battling a case of mono and the fallout of a failed romantic relationship, coupled with the dissolution of his old band, Vernon exiled himself from his Raleigh, North Carolina, home to spend the winter alone at his father's cabin in the northwestern Wisconsin woods. While there he wrote and recorded every track on *For Emma*, self-releasing it to wide acclaim in 2007. Kanye heard "Woods," the standout track from the *Blood Bank* EP, and wanted to sample it on *MBDTF*. As Vernon relates in the interview, "[Kanye] was like, 'I like how you sing so fearlessly. You don't care how your voice sounds. It'd be awesome if you could come out to Hawaii and hear the track...' I said, 'When should I come out?' And he said, 'How about tomorrow?'...So I head out there and he plays me ["Lost in the World"] and it sounds exactly like how you want it to sound: forward moving, interesting, light-hearted, heavy-hearted, fucking incredible sounding jam. It was kind of bare so I added some choir-sounding stuff and then thicked out the sample with my voice."

"Woods" is the harrowing final track on *Blood Bank*. Lyrically it comprises just four stark lines repeated like a depressive's mantra: "I'm up in the woods / I'm down on my mind / I'm building a still / To slow down the time." The song is a sonic hallucination occurring in the deepest parts of the self. It begins with the gingerly pace of someone carrying live ordnance across a minefield. Vernon's a cappella voice caresses each word with the utmost care, as though to stray even slightly from the prescribed syllables would mean annihilation. The first few vigilant iterations of the mantra feel like a test of the singer's stewardship, a spiritual rite of passage that, once complete, will grant him access to the song's holiest mysteries. Vernon uses a vocoder to achieve this effect through the subtle and steadily accreting attenuation of his voice. Layering the mantra upon itself in various unnatural pitches and levels of falsetto distortion, the singer's voice by song's end has evolved into an array of harmoniously emergent phenomena – an angel, a wolf, a ghost, a monk, and a baby among them – all of which are emanations of the voice's sudden self-discovery that it contains multitudes. There is a metamorphic power in the words, yes, but also in their persistence – in the voice's faith that salvation will eventually occur through disciplined repetition. The song's mystery is the mystery of self-transformation in solitude, an allegory of exile's capacity to broaden the spirit and remake the mind.

"Lost in the World" echoes the multitudes found deep within "Woods," but it does so by a miracle of imaginative transubstantiation. The intro begins almost exactly like that of "Woods," with the same supplicating voice (albeit in a slightly higher pitch) offering up its mantra/prayer to the infinite wilderness. Once again we are in the territory of Dante's pilgrim, far from the straightforward path and acutely aware of our dislocation.

As samples in Kanye West songs go, this one is barely altered from its original state. The first forty-two seconds could even be mistaken for the ur-"Woods" by an incurious ear. It is only at the forty-three second mark that we know where we are – at the still point of Kanye's creative powers, the control room of his ego. In the transitional second between the sample's death and its reincarnation, its passage from "Woods" to "World," we bear witness to a sonic miracle, listening with rapt incredulity as Vernon's melted snow magically changes to a river of rosé. The genius of *MBDTF*'s narcissism lies in its regurgitation of the world as a sacred, gold-embossed, red leather reflection of itself. As gravity sucks the sampled voice downward into the abyss (the sound is not unlike Kubrick's HAL losing consciousness, that archetypal wheeze of digital devices shutting down), Kanye materializes to seize the "Woods" mantra and refashion it into a declaration of unconditional freedom. No longer a quiet prayer handled delicately by a seeker, the new lyrics – which replace "woods" with "world" and remake the image of pastoral solitude into an urban labyrinth – burst forth with the bombast of the true believer. The hook is alternately soaring and freefalling, a Greek chorus of carnal ambiguity, one voice commingling with many, all of them uncertain where things are headed. The song's sole verse features a transformational Kanye embracing that unknown and reconciling the album's contradictions (devil/angel, heaven/hell, lies/truth, freedom/jail, etc.), fusing them in a fever of literal consummation before chanting "mama-say-mama-sa-mama-makossa" (a pointed reference to Michael Jackson's sample in "Wanna Be Startin' Something" of Cameroonian musician Manu Dibanoga's 1972 afrobeat single "Soul Makossa") and making promises about bountiful sex in the afterlife. Amid the exhilaration of the verse's delivery it's easy to hear the end of Kanye's chant as "mama-Michael-son," a productive misprision that links *MBDTF* with *Thriller* in a line of literal ancestry.

The real thrill of "Lost in the World," though, the secret wish given fulfillment by the song's vertiginous plunge, is the coincidence of intention and execution. Needing to be an ungainsayable exclamation point on a perfect album – a truly *great* song sophisticated enough to assimilate and synthesize the album's palette of mixed yearnings – "Lost in the World" succeeds beyond doubt. Strategically placed at the exit of the young century's most ambitious pop record, the song's sound is impossibly large, containing within it the entire *MBDTF* genome. This idea is palpable in the ascending circular motion of the main verse, with Kanye manically fusing contradictions like stacked base pairs in a DNA molecule. This is an album obliquely about the genetics of pop music, after all, a document about the knowns and unknowable unknowns that go into production. Could any other song wrap things up so definitively?

"Lost in the World" samples five different artists to achieve the lushness of its sound. The "Woods" sample – still intact in its original form throughout the repeated hook, just more recessive – lends the song its essential melodic scaffolding, as discussed above. The "Soul Makossa" sample provides the aforementioned moment of Michael Jackson Zen, a final wink and nod to *Thriller*'s legacy at the moment of *MBDTF*'s own transcendence. Just past the one minute mark a much-mined sample of the Lyn Collins soul classic "Think (About It)" – immortalized by Rob Base and DJ E-Z Rock in their 1988 platinum hit "It Takes Two," with its signature "Yeah! Woo!" squeal as recognizable today as ever (and used to a different end in "So Appalled") – joins the combustible hook of house beats, tribal drums, gospel-choir-styled backing vocals, and chanting. Add to that mix the opening drum break from Eddie Bo's "Hook and Sling – Part I" and you begin to get a sense of the song's thickness and complexity. The fifth and final sample, one that has the literal last word on the album, is an excerpt of Gil Scott-Heron's "Comment #1," wherein the pleading unanswerable question – "Who will survive in America?" – makes an intrusive cameo as "Lost in the World" downshifts into a thrum of tribal percussion and chants.

At this point it's worth noting that, technically speaking, "Lost in the World" is not the final track on *MBDTF*. That honor goes to a one minute thirty-eight second coda whose title – "Who Will Survive in America?" – comes from the Scott-Heron sample we hear poking holes in the end of "Lost in the World." As a rhetorical flourish wrapped in the same swirl of throbbing atmospherics, "Who Will Survive in

America?" is an extended meditation on "Lost in the World." The track comprises large chunks of Scott-Heron performing "Comment #1," composed in 1970 as a scathing indictment of the student-led New Left's racial and historical naiveté. The repurposed lines leave that context largely behind, serving instead to imbue the album's final moments with the legitimacy of social prophecy. More than one critic noted the incongruous melding of the two works – *MBDTF* is a narcissistic opera about one man's millions of contradictions; "Comment #1" is an acerbic plaint about the world-historical contradictions of racial injustice. What better means of putting a golden capstone on a work this narcissistic, though? In a record devoted to the idea of redemption through excess, to the notion that an ambitious enough ego can translate the universe into a song cycle of the self, the choice to feature "Comment #1" succeeds. The poem as recast in "Who Will Survive in America?" is one such translation, with Gil Scott-Heron's ghost ventriloquizing Kanye's angst and self-doubt. The existential uncertainty of the title, stripped from its original context, is no longer about the grim prospects for America's poorest citizens. The new uncertainty is about how and whether Kanye West will survive – as an artist, as a celebrity, as a man – and, should he make it, what kind of America would have him.

The *Yeezus* Singularity: A Religion of the Self

"What is this shit?"

As immortal rock criticism goes, the first four words in Greil Marcus' *Rolling Stone* review of *Self Portrait* are like the first four notes of Beethoven's Fifth – they contain all other generic possibilities. Marcus had spent the sixties vitalized by the evolution of Bob Dylan's genius, and *Self Portrait* arrived in 1970 like a dull fart punctuating Lincoln's Second Inaugural. What had happened? Dylan's first post-sixties album suddenly called into doubt what the critic and his like-minded friends held most sacred: "Were we really that impressionable back in '65, '66? Was it that the stuff really wasn't that good, that this is just as good? Was it some sort of accident in time that made those other records so powerful, or what?" An unfortunate axiom of both criticism and fandom is that, on a long enough timeline, even a definitive artist like Dylan will, inevitably, disappoint. If philosophy was born the moment man understood suicide to be a choice among other choices, genuine pop criticism begins and ends with the critic's admission that even the greatest artists are capable of making bad art. How do you follow up a decade of music as bold, ambitious, and generative as Dylan's sixties,

Michael's eighties, or Kanye's aughts? As a deviation from a burnished ideal, *Self Portrait* was disappointing in the way of all pop music disappointments. Time's funky march is always on parade, though, and the subsequent decades have transformed it into a fascinating meditation on the self-conscious limits of Dylan's multiplicity and minstrelsy. Michael Jackson released 1991's *Dangerous*, another record time has refashioned into an appreciating asset, an undervalued snapshot of a pop titan at a racially fraught cultural and historical crossroads. How do you follow an album as close to "perfect," though, as *MBDTF*? If you're Kanye West, you negate it.

To promote the release of *Yeezus*, his sixth studio album, Kanye managed to conflate performance art with projectile narcissism through an ingenious global conceit. On the Friday before his featured appearance as musical guest on the May 18, 2013 broadcast of *Saturday Night Live*, he tweeted:

NEW SONG AND VISUAL FROM MY NEW ALBUM BEING PROJECTED TONIGHT ACROSS THE GLOBE ON 66 BUILDINGS, LOCATIONS @ KANYEWEST.COM

His website offered visitors a cryptically simple black map of the globe with tiny red dots representing each of the ten cities where projections would take place. The graphic had the minimalist grimness of a Soviet nuclear war protocol, which was precisely the point. Clicking the red dot on Chicago, for example, yielded the various times and locations (Wrigley Field among them) where the "song and visual" would strike. The track at the heart of this campaign was "New Slaves," an interesting but ham-fisted diatribe on the

Jim Crow antinomies of hyper-conspicuous consumerism. The projection featured a stark, enormous black and white image of West's face, a thick gold chain around his neck. A random passerby could have been forgiven for mistaking the event as a Mr. T publicity stunt, the *A-Team* alum reincarnated as Big Brother in a guerrilla marketing campaign for toothpaste. The video projections were a lot more than mere commercial ploys, however. They were never intended to foster a sense of local or global community, or to collapse the tremendous distances between cities and people. They were performances of that distance, a stylized estrangement of commodity from consumer. With *MBDTF* Kanye re-established his place in pop music, and *Yeezus* is his back-biting and ungenerous manifesto from the mountain peak, twenty-first century pop music's anti-Sermon on the Mount. It bears the unique honor of being the only *underproduced* album in his oeuvre, Rick Rubin's contributions to the record notwithstanding. Search for a nook or corner of warmth on *Yeezus*, a space for tapping into the kind of orchestral possibility that defines Kanye's best music – you won't find one. (A possible exception is "Bound 2," which owes its human element to two incredible samples: the guileless teenage melody of 1971's "Bound" by the Ponderosa Twins Plus One, punctuated with a one-second come-hither Brenda Lee moan of approbation – "Uh huh, Honey!" – from her 1959 single "Sweet Nothin's.") Critics gushed over Daft Punk's contributions to the album's serrated post-industrial sound – all the buzzsaw bleeps and bloops and sonic laser beams and roboticized synth drones. Even the late, great Lou Reed, whose *Metal Machine Music* – the *Yeezus* of its time – had tortured Lester Bangs so mercilessly way back in 1975, penned a generous review for *Talkhouse* magazine:

> Very often, he'll have this very monotonous section going and then, suddenly — 'BAP! BAP! BAP! BAP!' — he disrupts the whole thing and we're on to something new that's absolutely incredible. That's architecture, that's structure — this guy is seriously smart. He keeps unbalancing you. He'll pile on all this sound and then suddenly pull it away, all the way to complete silence, and then there's a scream or a beautiful melody, right there in your face. That's what I call a sucker punch.

Hailed though it was by virtually every major critical outlet, landing at the top of dozens of year-end lists, *Yeezus* seemed to me upon first listen to be hollow, rushed, unfelt – a hurried response to an unspoken dare. Reed addresses that notion in his review, but he examines it from a standpoint of awe: "And now, with this album, it's 'Now that you like me, I'm going to make you *unlike* me.' It's a dare. It's braggadocio. Axl Rose has done that too, lots of people have. 'I Am a God' – I mean, with a song title like that, he's just *begging* people to attack him."

These days, it's almost impossible to hear or see the word "unlike" without connotations of Facebook's binary toggle switch of endorsement/estrangement, and, for Reed, that's why the album's gambit is so successful. "Kanye West is a child of social media and hip hop," Reed begins his review. But isn't a bet made against your "audience" (social media's *raison d'être*) an act of bad faith? We know that Yeezy is driven by an ever more complicated self-conception of capital "A" art. Can a concept album's *concept* be a gestural "fuck-you," and does that choice – in its sheer anti-commercial rudeness – make it somehow more *artistic* than an artist's other records? Is *Yeezus* a performance piece, the minimalist jewel case album cover (more accurately, *lack* of an album cover, bound shut with a piece of red tape) a comment on the emptiness of what's inside, a reflection of our depthless culture's indiscriminate hunger for new content? Or, equally plausible, is *Yeezus* just a half-baked turd casserole, its hype the disingenuous enthusiasm of a salesman whose fervor for his wares belies their certain inferiority? These are not easy questions, especially given the thrilling productivity of West's previous engagement with established artists. If *MBDTF* achieved nothing else, it earned its creator the benefit of our doubt regarding questions of artistic intention. One may harbor suspicions that the music on *Yeezus* is arbitrary or bankrupt of vision, but we owe it to Kanye's genius to at least conduct a thorough investigation.

And so when the album leaked four days early on June 14, 2013, I listened all the way through, and then I listened again. I listened on the treadmill, and I listened in the car on the way to meet my wife at childbirth class. Just over a week later, our son was born. The twinkling, heart-swollen hook of "Return to Pooh Corner" immediately replaced the "gnarled dancehall vocal sample and paranoid sawtooth synths" (as Ryan Dombal wrote reviewing *Yeezus* for Pitchfork) of "I Am a God." During the subsequent days and weeks, on the rare occasions when lullabies weren't streaming from every speaker, a few songs on the album ("Blood on the Leaves," "Black Skinhead," "Handle My Liquor") got better with each listen. On balance, though, *Yeezus* still felt irresolute and noncommittal, an exercise in aesthetic contempt or – perhaps more accurately – the onset of a contemptuous aesthetic. Kanye deemed the sound "aspirational minimalism" in interviews, and he may be on to something. It is music that aspires to a kind of libidinal void – a whorl of affective blankness – and I didn't like it at all.

Again, the timeless question returned: *What is this shit?*

Nashville's Bridgestone Arena is an immense glass and concrete structure whose design could have been taken from one of the sci-fi comic books George McFly reads in *Back to the Future*. A cantilevered dome rests atop the arena's rectangular fortress, abutted in the front by a glass turret on top of which a radio tower ascends like a spaceman's helmet antenna. Home to the NHL's Nashville Predators and one of the busiest venues in North America, the arena has hosted everything from big ticket acts like Taylor Swift and Lady Gaga to the U.S. Gymnastics championships to the Country Music Association (CMA) Awards. On the bitterly cold Wednesday night before Thanksgiving 2013 – while millions of my fellow Americans had already begun drinking in earnest as preparation for a weekend of extended family – my mother-in-law Ruth and I stood in line to get our tickets scanned at the entrance. The *Yeezus* Tour had found its way to Music City, and we were there to be witnesses.

We certainly weren't the only ones, but the crowd was far from capacity. During Kendrick Lamar's dynamic Compton Roadshow opening performance, we wondered whether the multiple bald spots around the arena – the rows upon rows of empty seats – would fill up when Yeezus himself descended from Pop Heaven. More people did arrive later, but not enough to counter the feeling that Kanye – easily the most important artist of his generation – was unappreciated in a city whose chamber of commerce trumpets Nashville's musical eclecticism and "It City" status at every available opportunity. This was more complex than the city's calcified grudge over the Swift incident, or the inconvenience of a concert falling on the night before a major American holiday, or even the fact that Corrections Corporation of America (CCA) – name-checked as a social scourge on "New Slaves" – is headquartered in Nashville. Like the boos he received at the Dodgers game a few months earlier when his image flashed across the jumbotron, the unfilled seats were an expression of collective social disgust, an (ironic) rejection of the idea that narcissism is a proper religion. The erstwhile rap nerd in the Dropout Bear suit had anointed himself a Christ of culture, and now he had come to descend like Zarathustra onto the buckle of the Bible Belt with his message of holy transformation.

The various *Yeezus* Tour T-shirts on sale in the arena – a few of which featured some combination of a death's head, the Confederate flag, and redneck secessionist sloganeering ("I AIN'T COMIN' DOWN") – gave form to this idea. Here was one of the most controversial and successful black artists of all time, playing one of the most heavily trafficked venues in the South – a location just a stone's throw from where the lunch counter sit-ins had occurred more than half a century earlier – and on sale at his merch table were gonzo caricatures of the nation's racist past. The painful symbol of America's original sin had been expropriated, rebranded, and

MY BEAUTIFUL DARK TWISTED FANTASY

commodified – $35 a pop – an object lesson in the power of cultural capital and the ahistorical force of Kanye's ego. Like Elvis's capacity to unmake himself with a joke during his comeback special in 1968, Kanye's ability to turn the Confederate flag into a personal logo is a testament to his power. On more than one occasion during the *Yeezus* Tour, the artist referred to himself in interviews as the "nucleus of culture." The flag shirts tested the limits of that nuclear power, cramming his abiding fascinations – the mass commercialization of avant-garde fashion, the idea of provocation as a personal brand, the divorce of personal intention from social consequence – down the throat of a receptive mainstream. Asked about the controversy surrounding the shirts on Los Angeles radio station 97.1 AMP, West said: "You know the Confederate flag represented slavery in a way – that's my abstract take on what I know about it. So I made the song 'New Slaves.' So I took the Confederate flag and made it my flag. It's my flag. Now what are you going to do?"

The performance that night at Bridgestone Arena was a revelation, the clarification of my own dimly apprehended ideas about the music on *Yeezus*. The Internet had been overflowing with images of the show's Wagnerian theatrics – the towering white mountain and the protruding glacier; the ashen-haired demon with glowing red eyes that paces anxiously at a distance; the harem of women wearing translucent masks, white acolyte vestments, and flesh-toned body stockings; the orgiastic evocation of the Sistine Chapel ceiling; Kanye's multiple bejeweled face masks; black and white projections of gerunds like "FIGHTING" and

"FALLING" with eerie, inscrutable definitions; the appearance of a Caucasian Jesus Christ – but I was unprepared for their cumulative effect. The visual conceit of the Maison Martin Margiela masks Kanye sported for most of his performance signified something along the lines of, as *Rolling Stone* put it, "look not upon the face of Yeezus, mere mortals." The genre-melting poet of narcissism has set his sights far beyond the bounds of pop music, and *Yeezus* – as song cycle, as persona, as prophecy – is the next evolutionary leap forward. During the middle of the show, West delivered an unscripted sermon while the motif from "Runaway" looped softly in the background. Though many in the audience were visibly flummoxed, irritated by an unexpected stoppage in the show's machinery, I was thrilled. This was "Sinners in the Hands of an Angry Mogul," Yeezus among the lowly speaking not about gentleness or humility but lambasting corporate elitism as an impediment to his creative omnipotence. He made headlines that night by calling out Mark Parker, CEO of Nike, for declining to bring Kanye's Air Yeezy sneakers to market. Animating the harangue was the fury of a thwarted child, a creatively pure entity of limitless imagination who cannot fathom the cruelty of a world with limits. My difficulties trying to understand and love *Yeezus* had been frustrated by my conviction that records made only one demand – to be loved. Certainly many do exist to be loved, but many more demand to make money, or draw boundaries, or win friends. What Kanye wants and what *Yeezus* demands, I finally understood watching the show, is a life of frictionless self-expression, a harmonic convergence between all of his "dreams" and the myriad gaps in the marketplace waiting to house them. *Yeezus* is a manifesto dedicated to that imperative, the crumpling-metal sound of his total commitment to a religion of Kanye West.

As he scaled the white mountaintop on stage and raised his hands to the heavens – 2-D storm clouds skittering above him on an enormous circular projection screen – Kanye was full of godlike defiance as the familiar intro to "POWER" blared. An arena in a mid-sized southern city had been transformed into one man's berserk Valhalla. Less than a half hour into his performance, and everyone felt the same sensation of mystery, the hunch that anything could happen next.

Here's to more of that feeling.

Also available in the series

ALSO AVAILABLE IN THE SERIES

ALSO AVAILABLE IN THE SERIES